School's Out For Teachers

JAMES STILES PHOTOGRAPHY

stilesphotography.com

School's Out For Teachers
SCHOOL STAFF PORTRAITS
J A M E S   S T I L E S   P H O T O G R A P H Y

INTRODUCTION:

I began this portrait project in the first half of the 2019-20 school year before it was suddenly cut short by the pandemic, returning to it in the 2022-23 school year (without masks.)

My hope is to show the three dimensionality and richness of these individuals beyond the school day, providing a small glimpse of their personal worlds. I'm told through showing these images that many of the staff are also getting to know each other a bit better for it (their hobbies, passions, accomplishments & dreams.)

To create this, I had asked the PVPHS High School staff to bring personal inanimate things to be photographed with. These things did not have to be totally self-defining. They could be whimsical things as well or some sport or hobby enjoyed, even a particular item of clothing, or a cherished object. The more that was brought to the photo shoot the more opportunities that gave me to do something creative with it.

Everyone in the book has signed releases and were given printed and digital photos from their shoot. Most have also provided a favorite quote to be displayed under their images. So far to date I have had 75 staff join in on this project.

Thank you to all who participated!

With love and respect,
James Stiles
PVPHS - Photo & Video Teacher
stilesj@pvpusd.net
jstilesphoto@gmail.com

This book is dedicated to my loving mother Pat Stiles who always encouraged creativity and the arts above all else.
It is also dedicated my wife Kie Salgado who supported and helped me through every step behind the scenes.

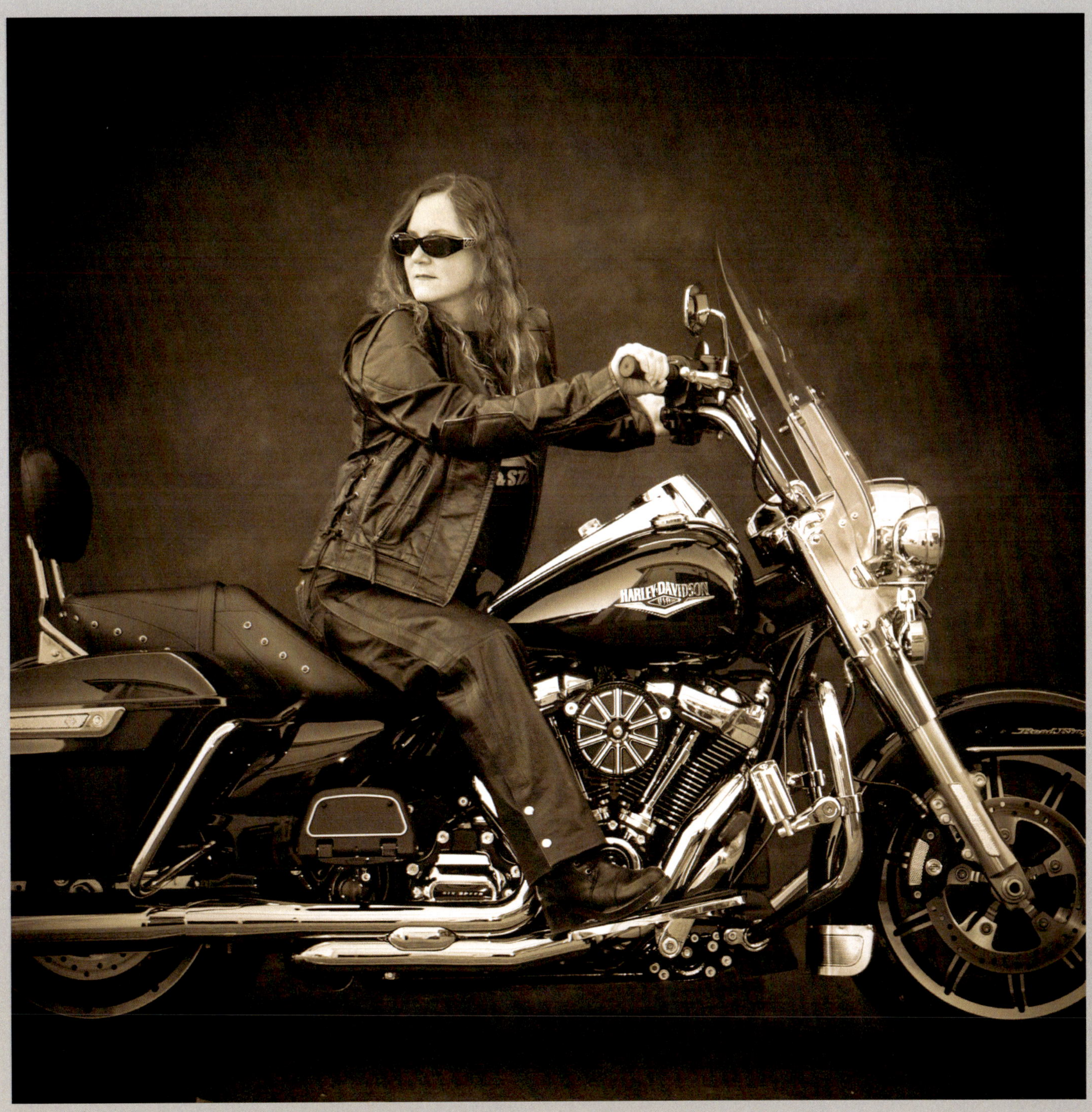

Colette Dunn-Kottke, *History Teacher.* -
"Do more things that make you smile."

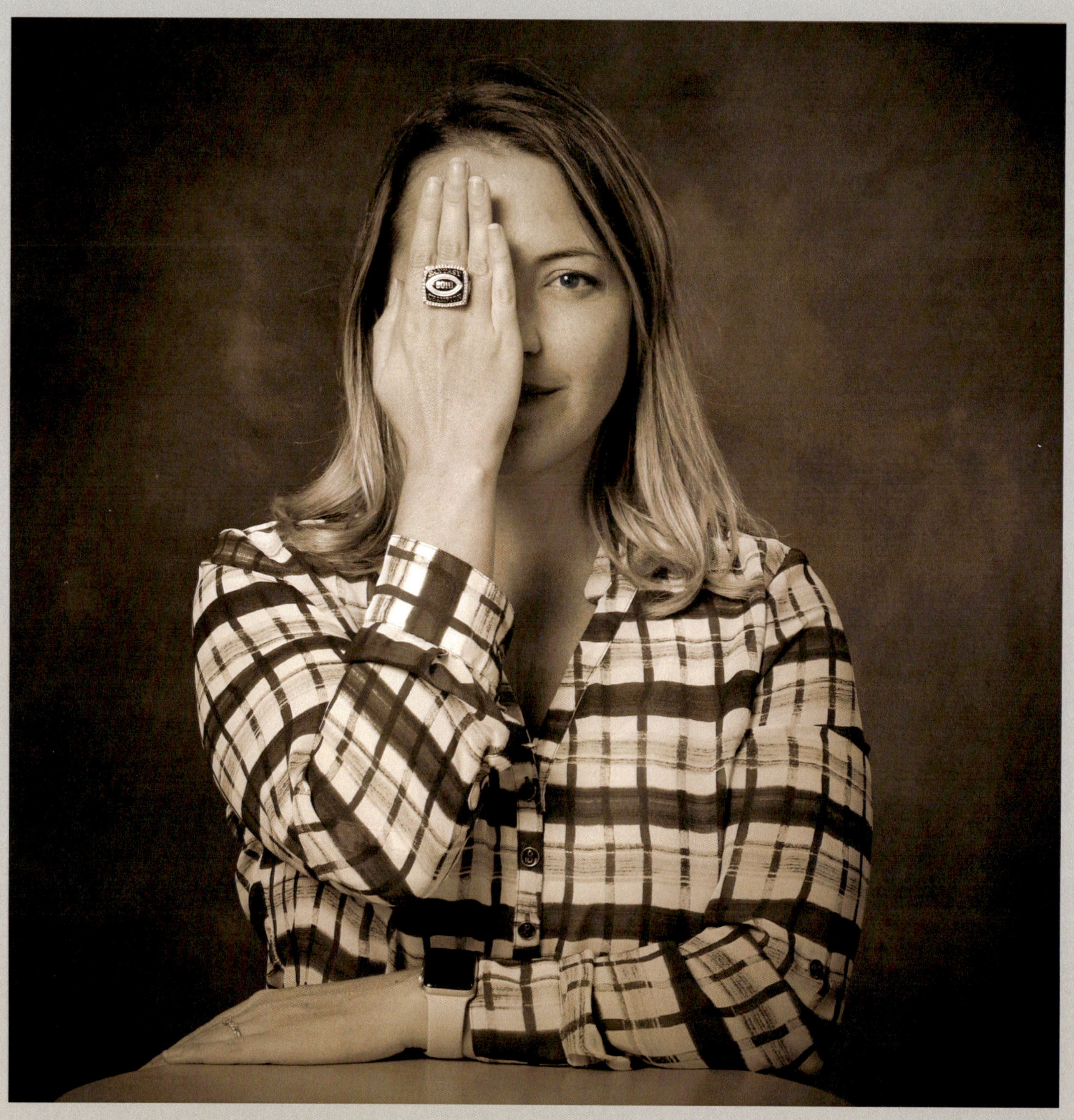

Katie Clovis, *Associate Principal.* -
"The winner takes it all. The loser's standing small. Beside the victory. That's her destiny." - ABBA

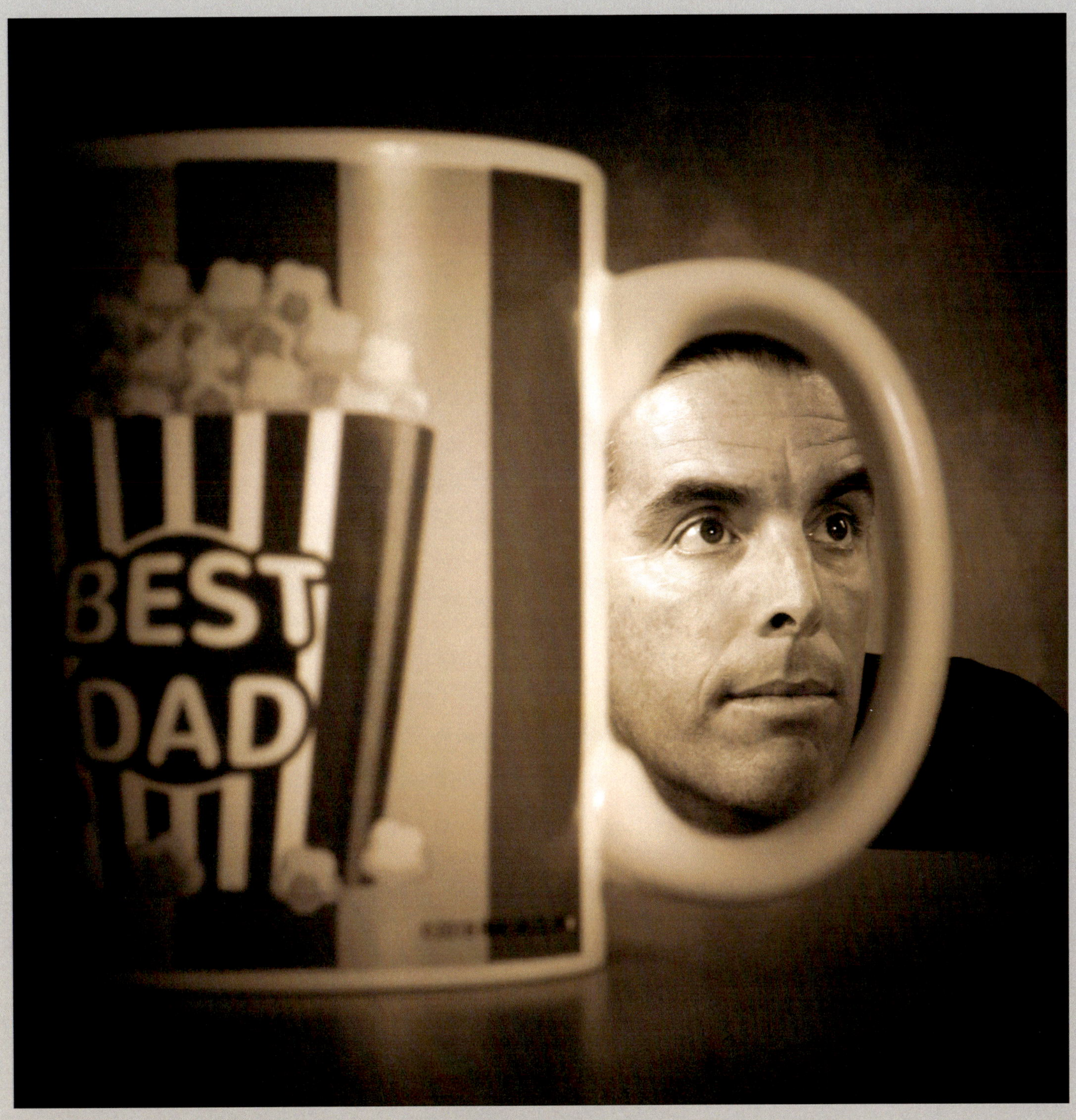

Brent Kuykendall, *Principal.* -
"I may be a principal now, but I will ALWAYS be a Dad first."

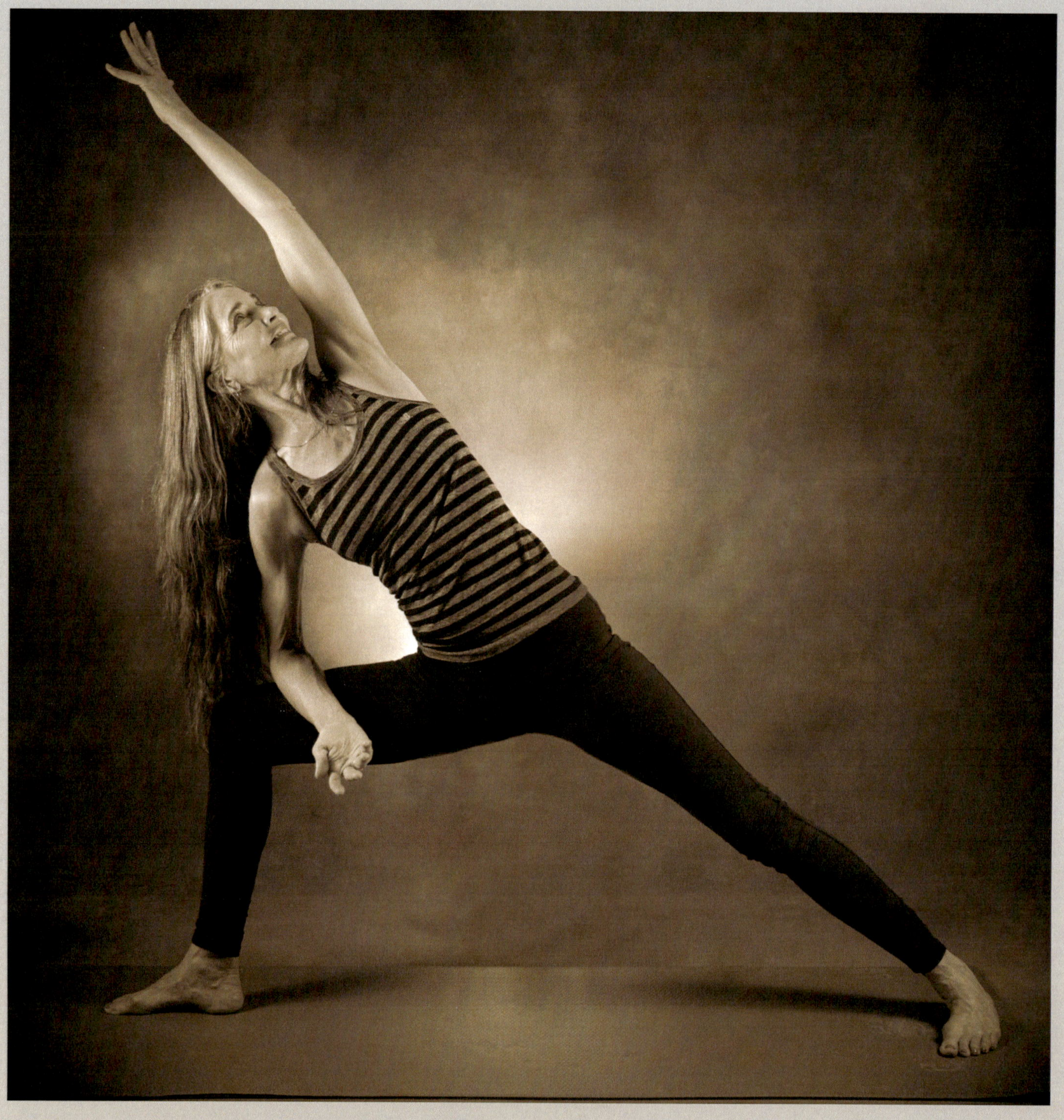

Anne Leonard, *Culinary Arts & Psychology Teacher.* -
"How wonderful it is that no one need wait a single moment before starting to improve the world." - Anne Frank

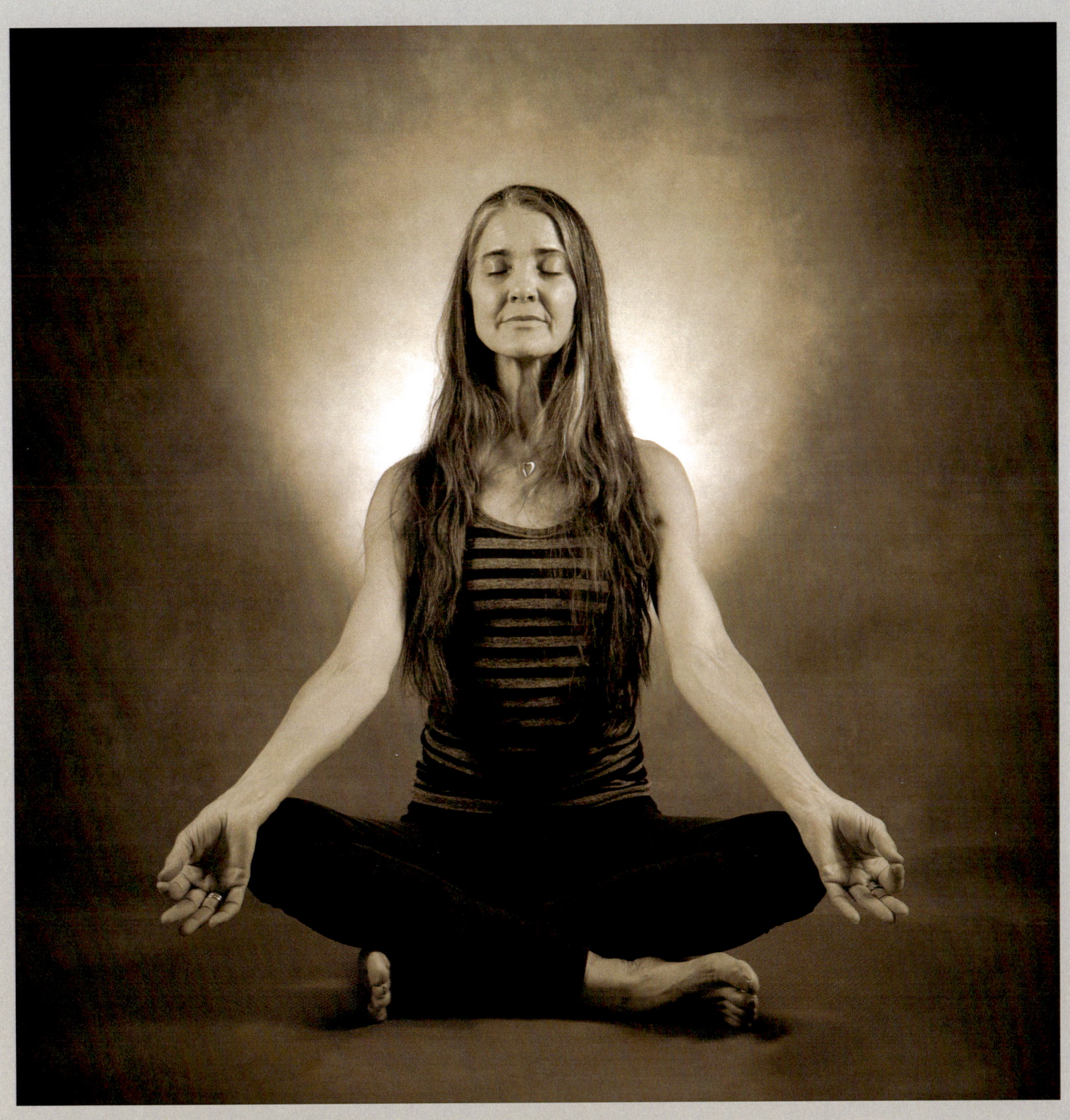

Anne Leonard, *Culinary Arts & Psychology Teacher.*

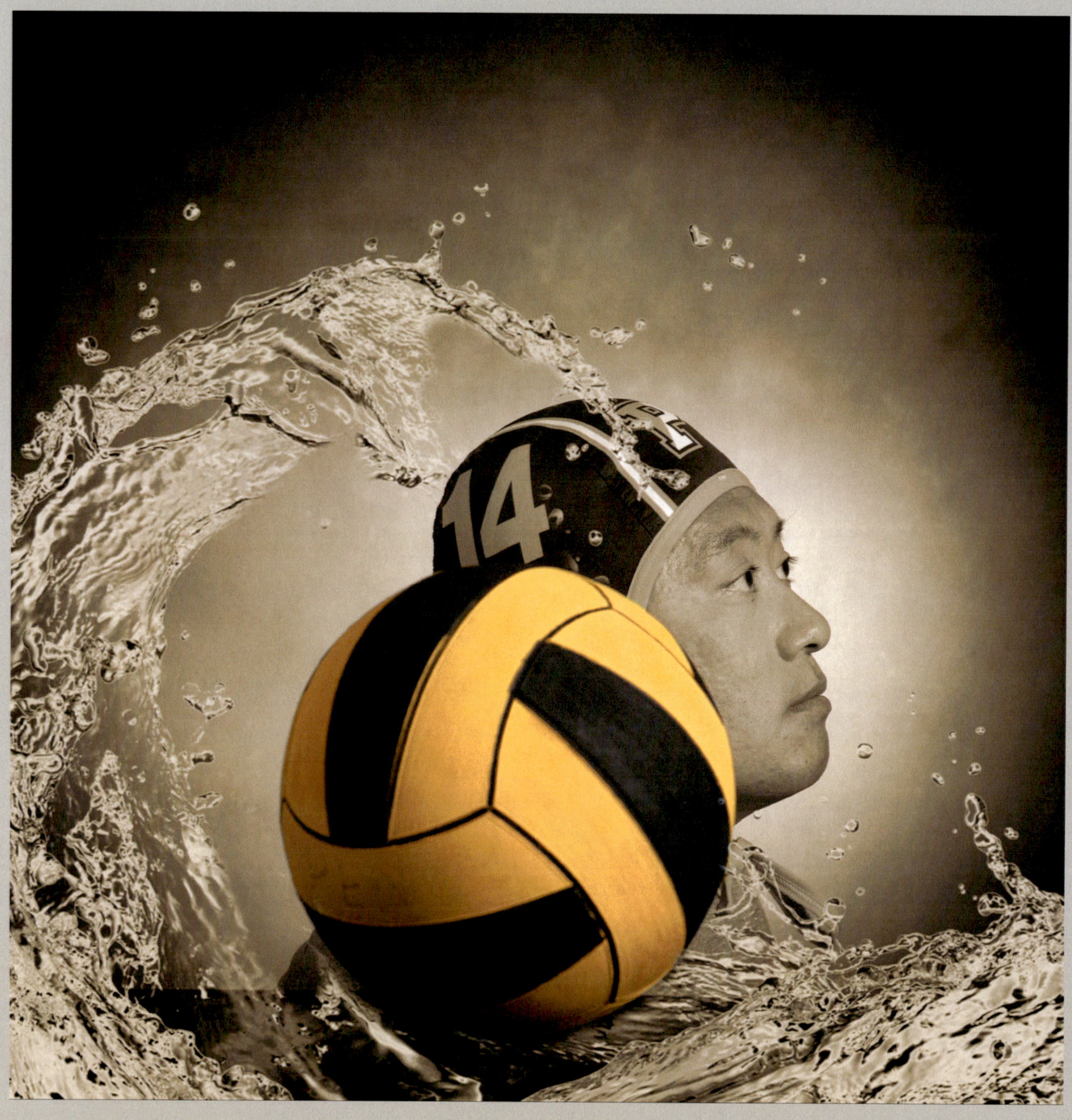

Charles Kim, *Water Polo Coach & World History Teacher.* -
"Passion is energy. Feel the power that comes from focusing on what excites you." - Oprah
Winfrey

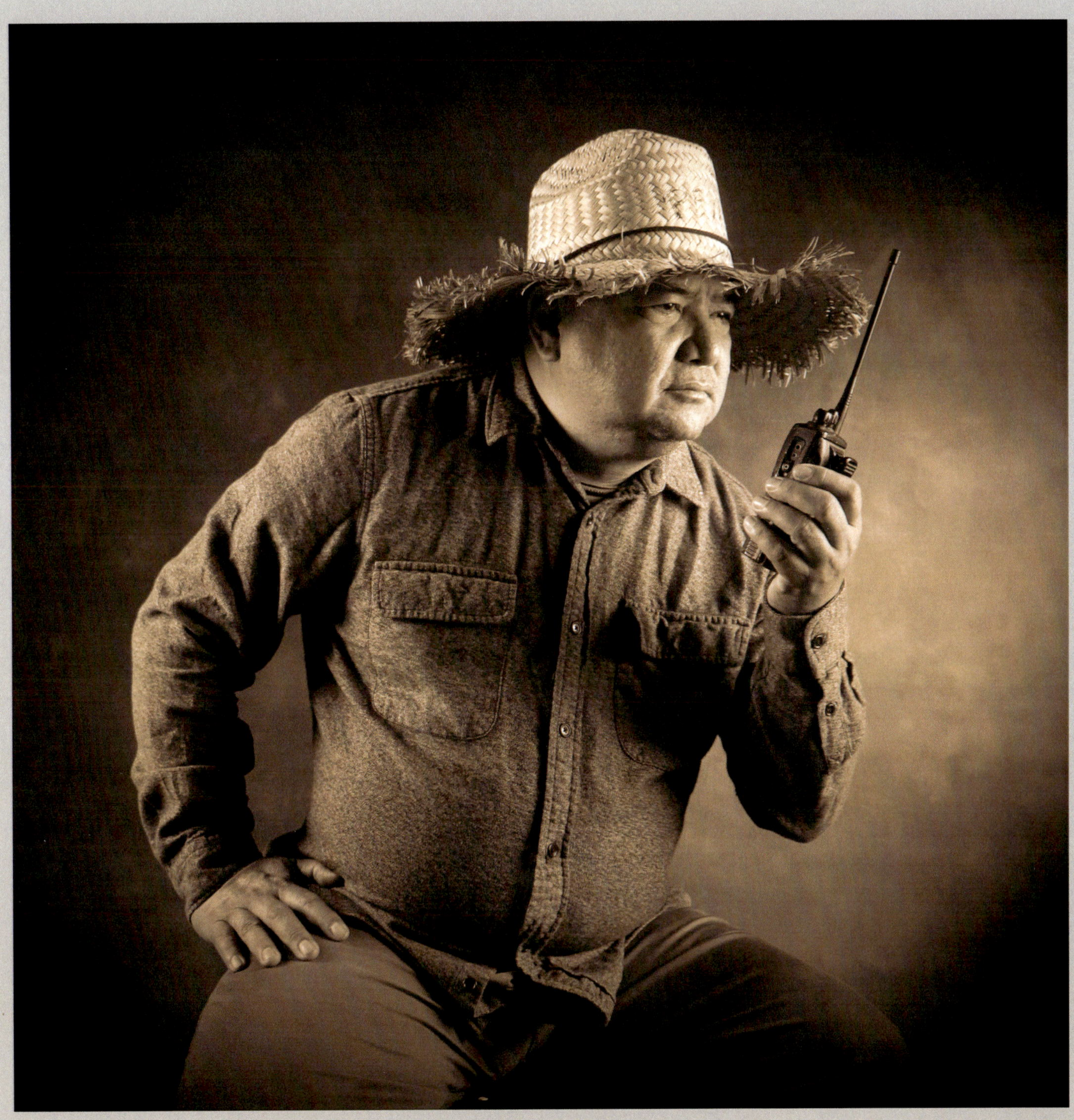

Al Liwig, *Head Custodian.* -
"Always here to serve."

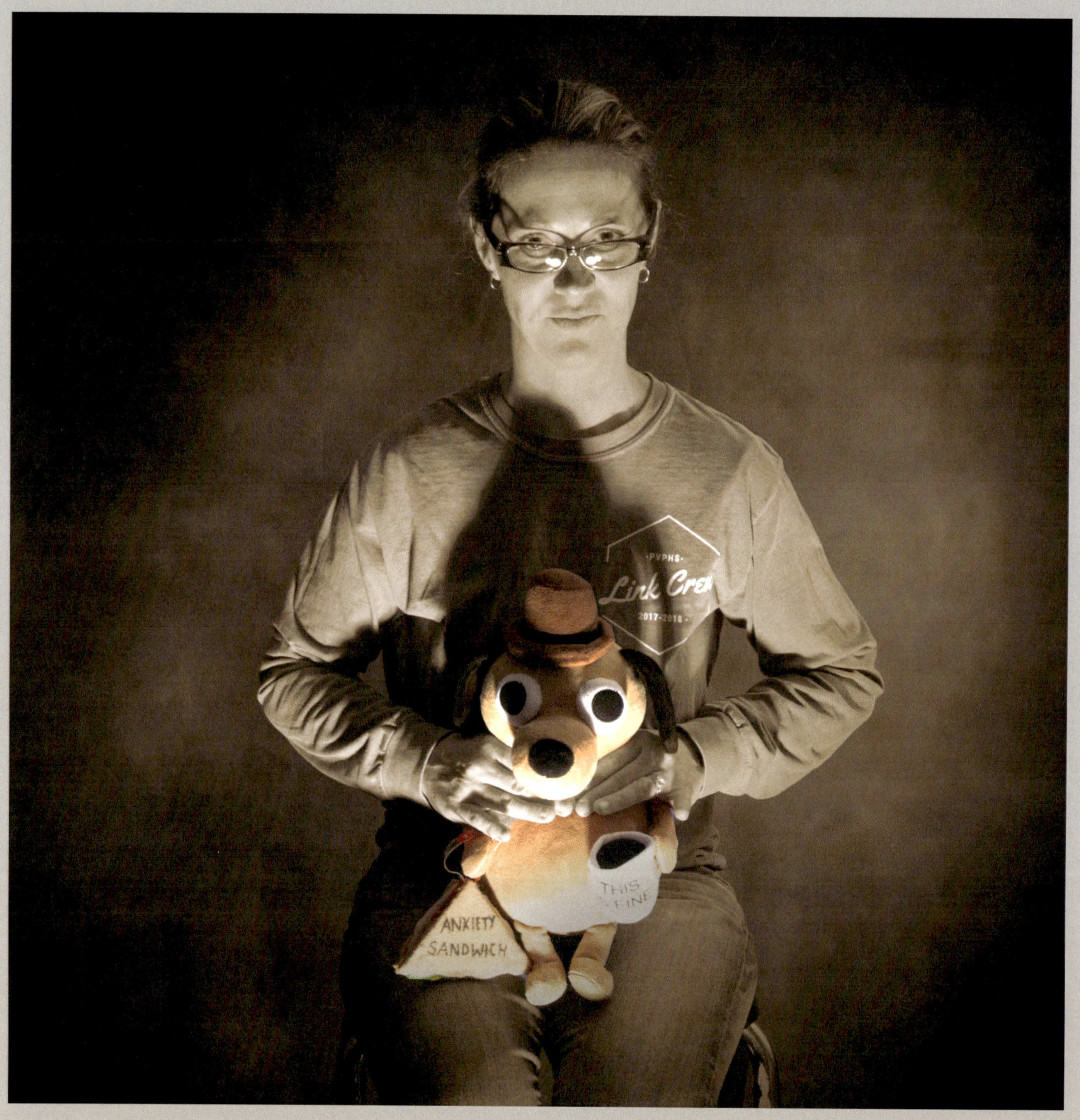

Beckie Dibble, *English Language Teacher.* -
"There's power in looking silly and not caring that you do." - Amy Poehler

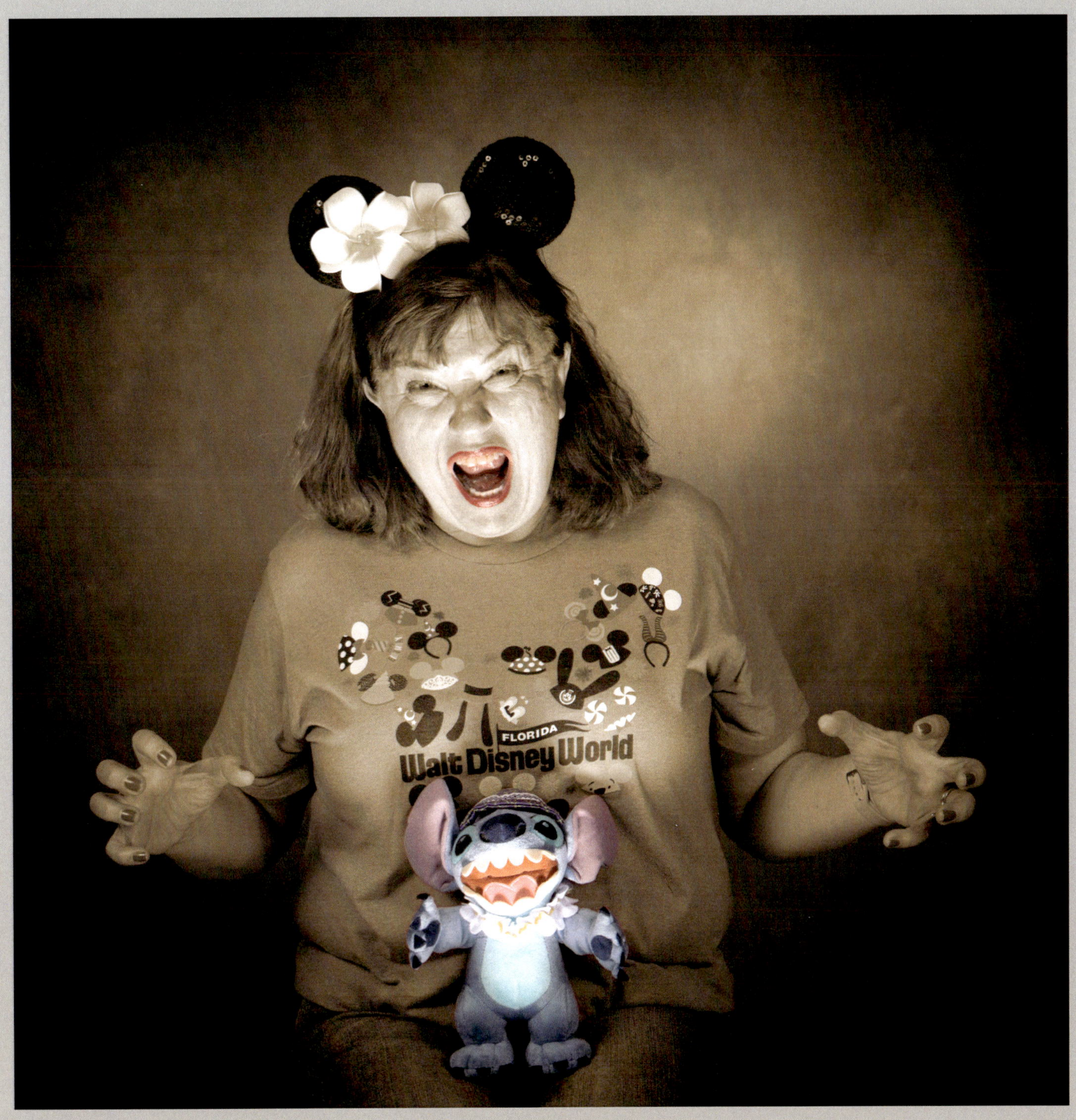

Betsy Okamoto, *English Language Teacher.* -
"Go confidently in the direction of your dreams! Live the life you've imagined."

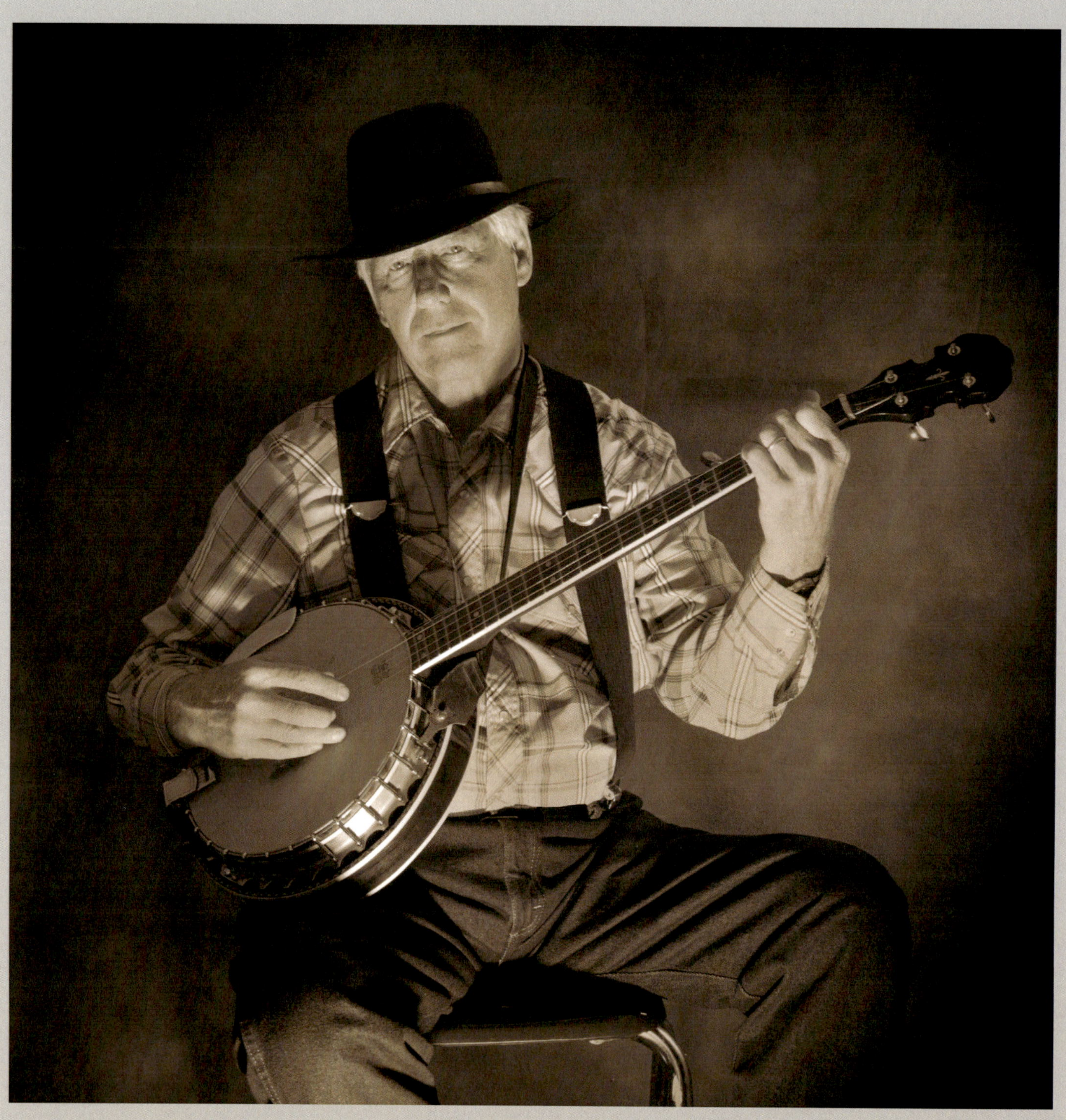

Mike Adyniec, *Math Teacher.*

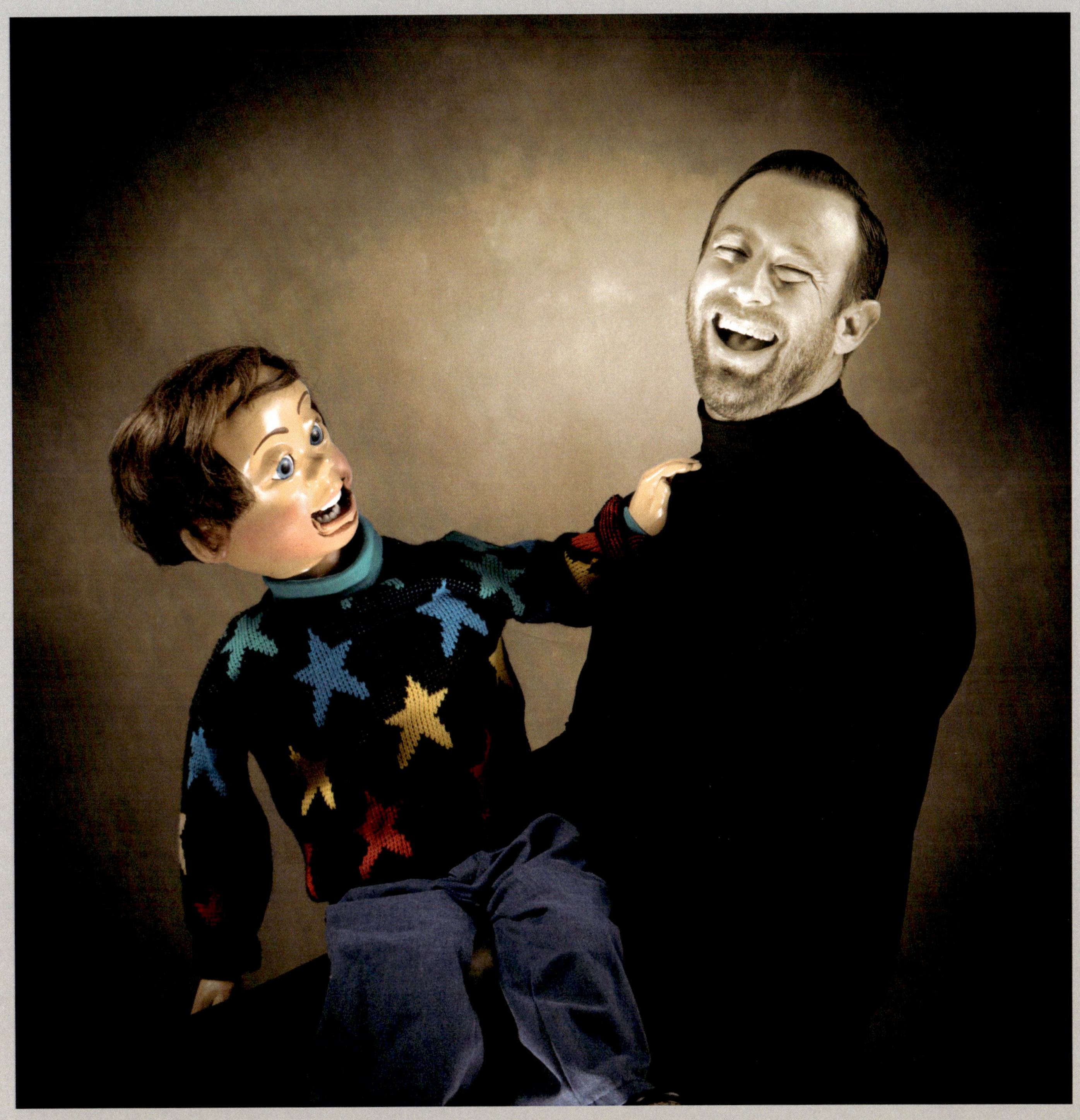

Adam Wolven, *Counselor.* -
"Nothing is scarier than a clown or ventriloquist dummy."

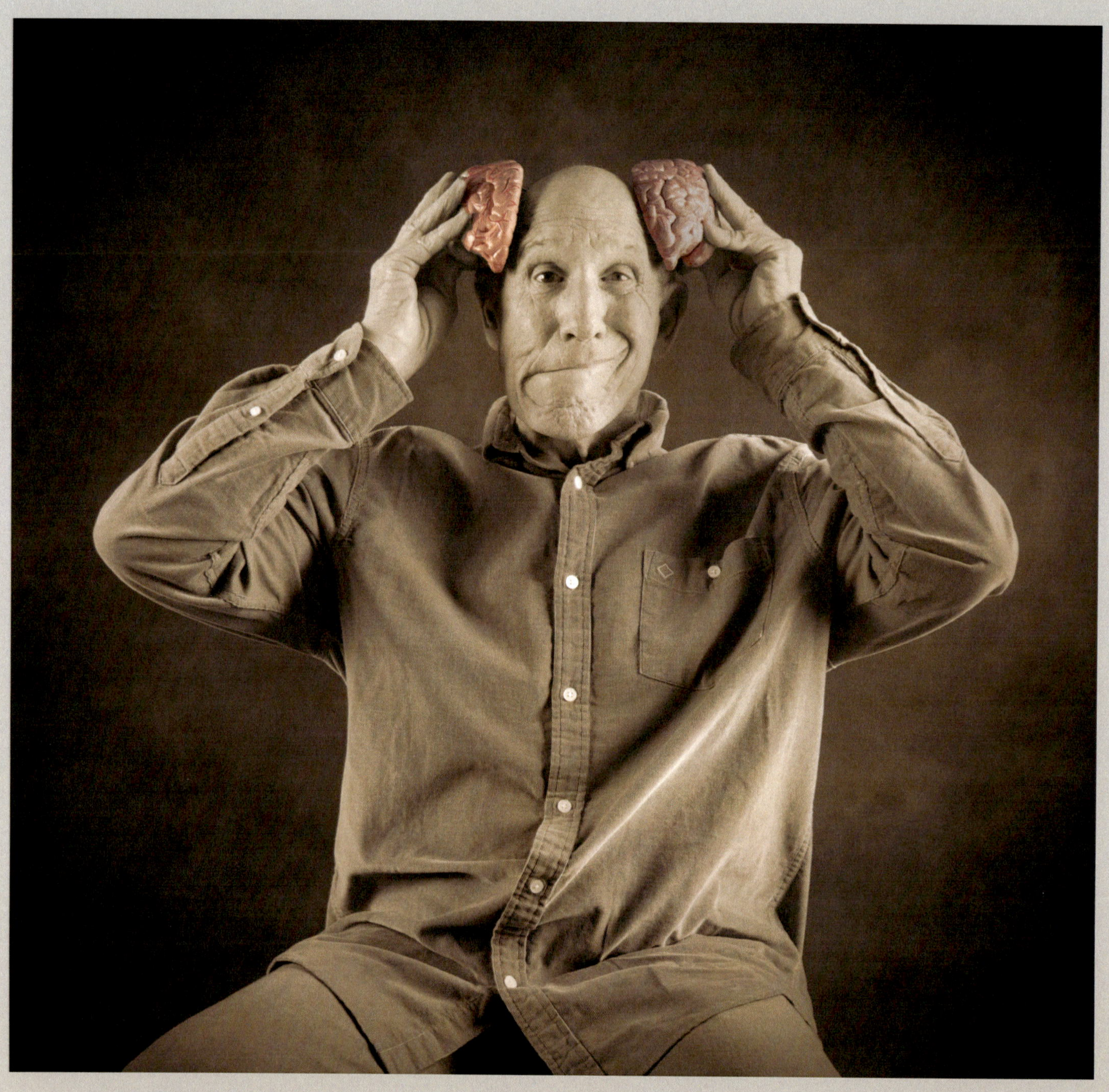

John Wheeler, *Psychology Teacher.* -
"Two heads are better than one."

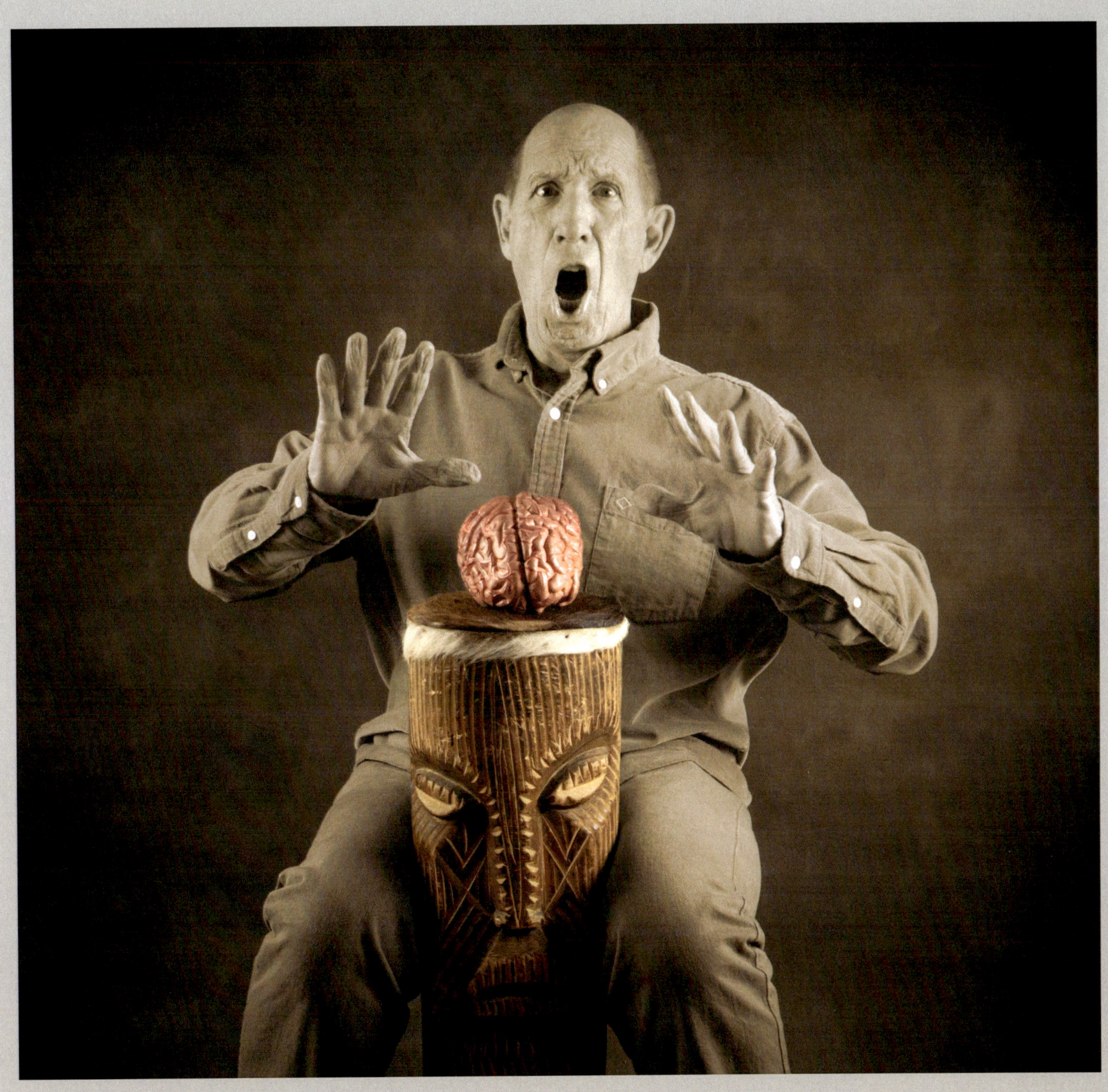

John Wheeler, *Psychology Teacher.*

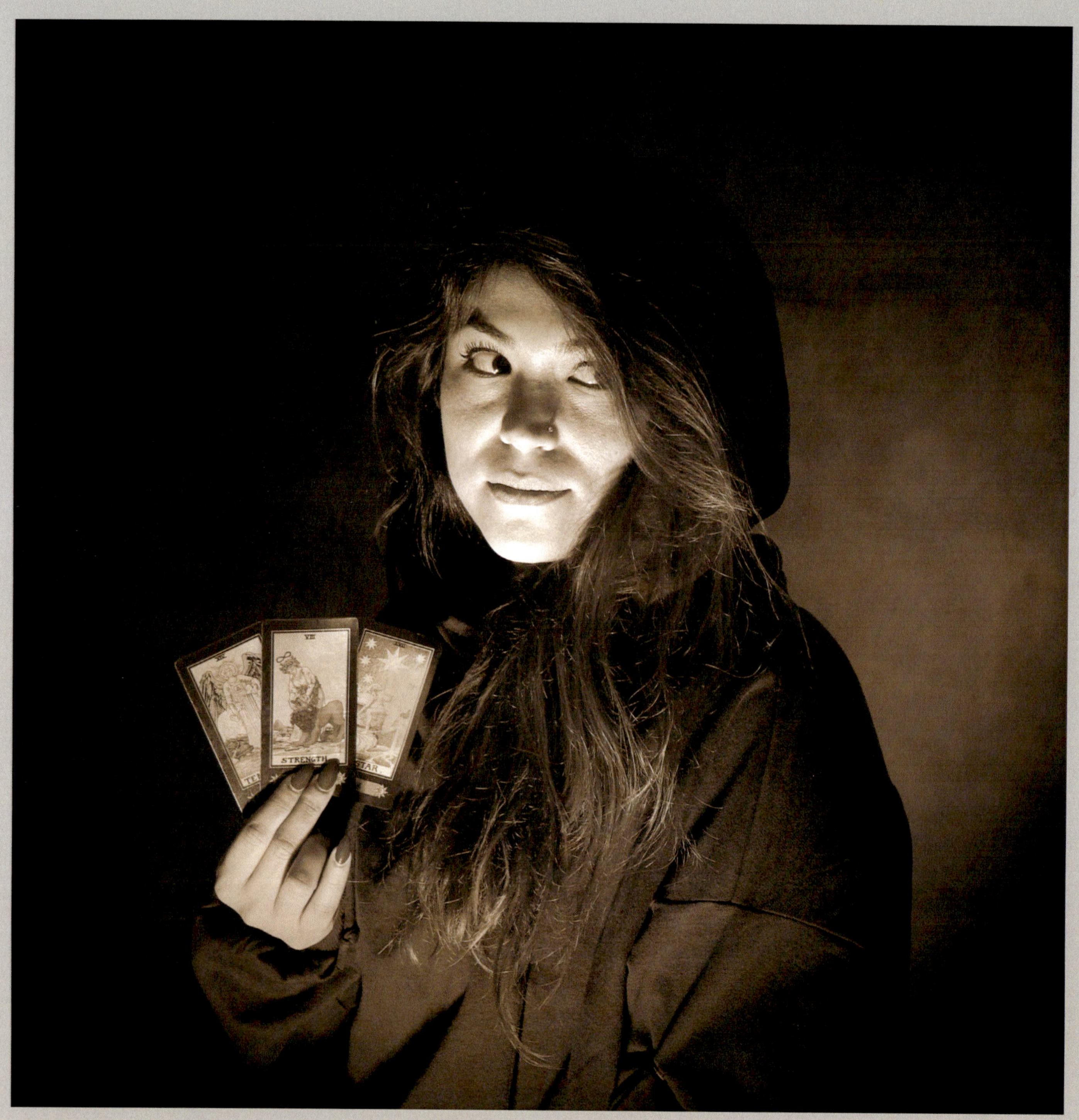

Brittni Rodriquez, *Student Aide*.

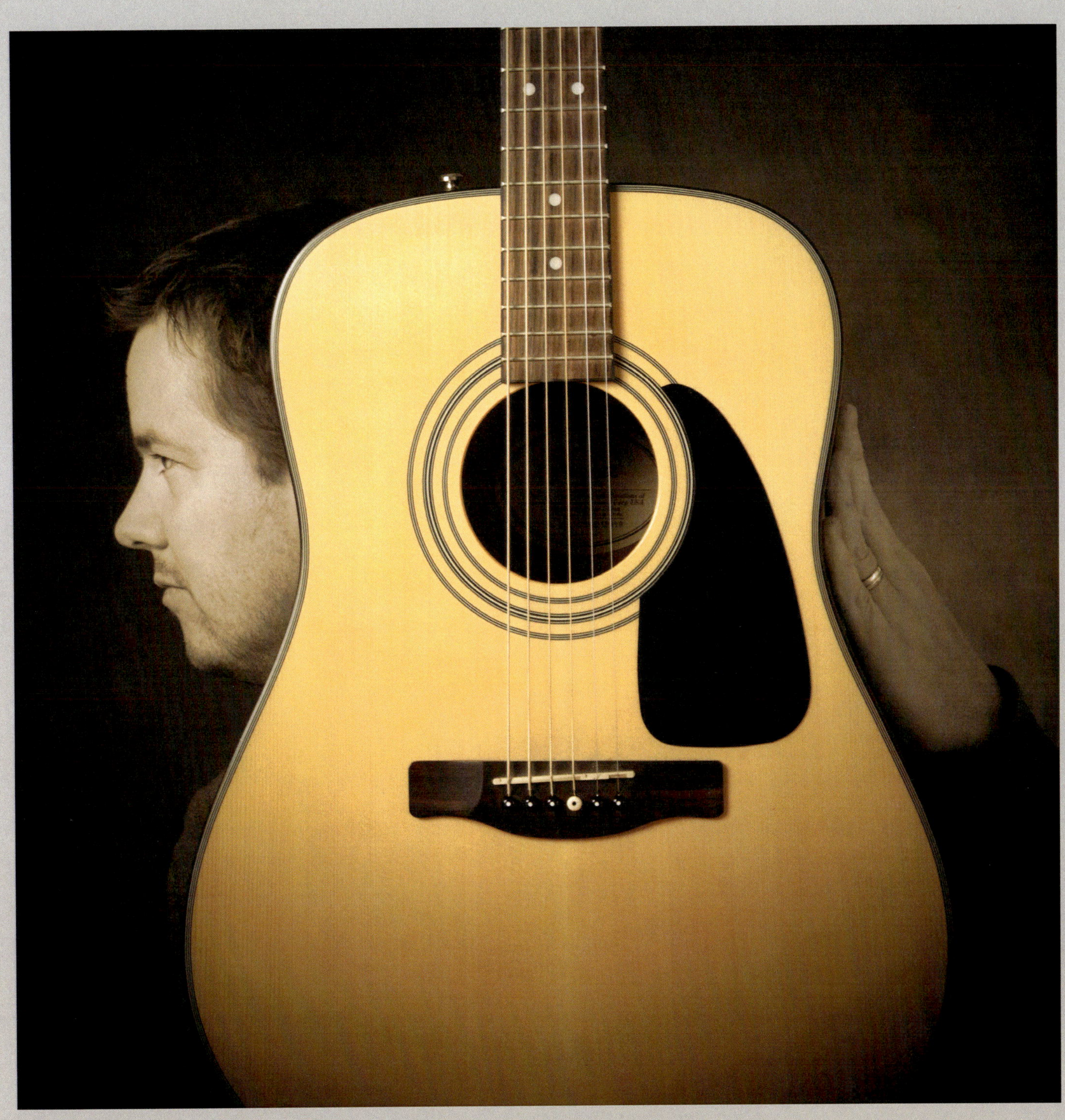

Dan Doctor, *Choir & AP Music Teacher.* -
"YOLO"

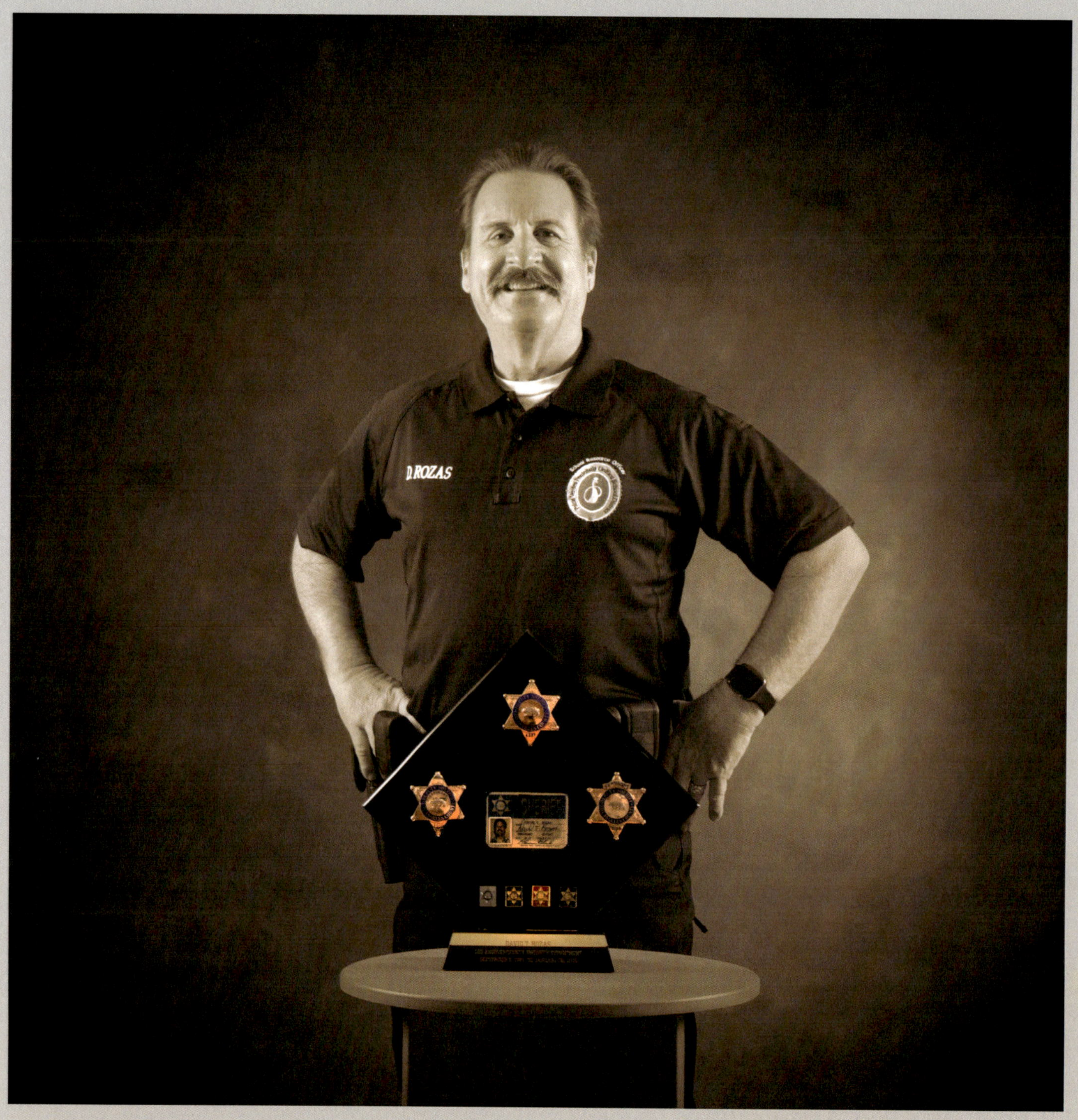

Dave Rozas, *School Resource Officer.* -
"Do not go where the path may lead, go instead where there is no path and leave a trail." -
Ralph Waldo Emerson

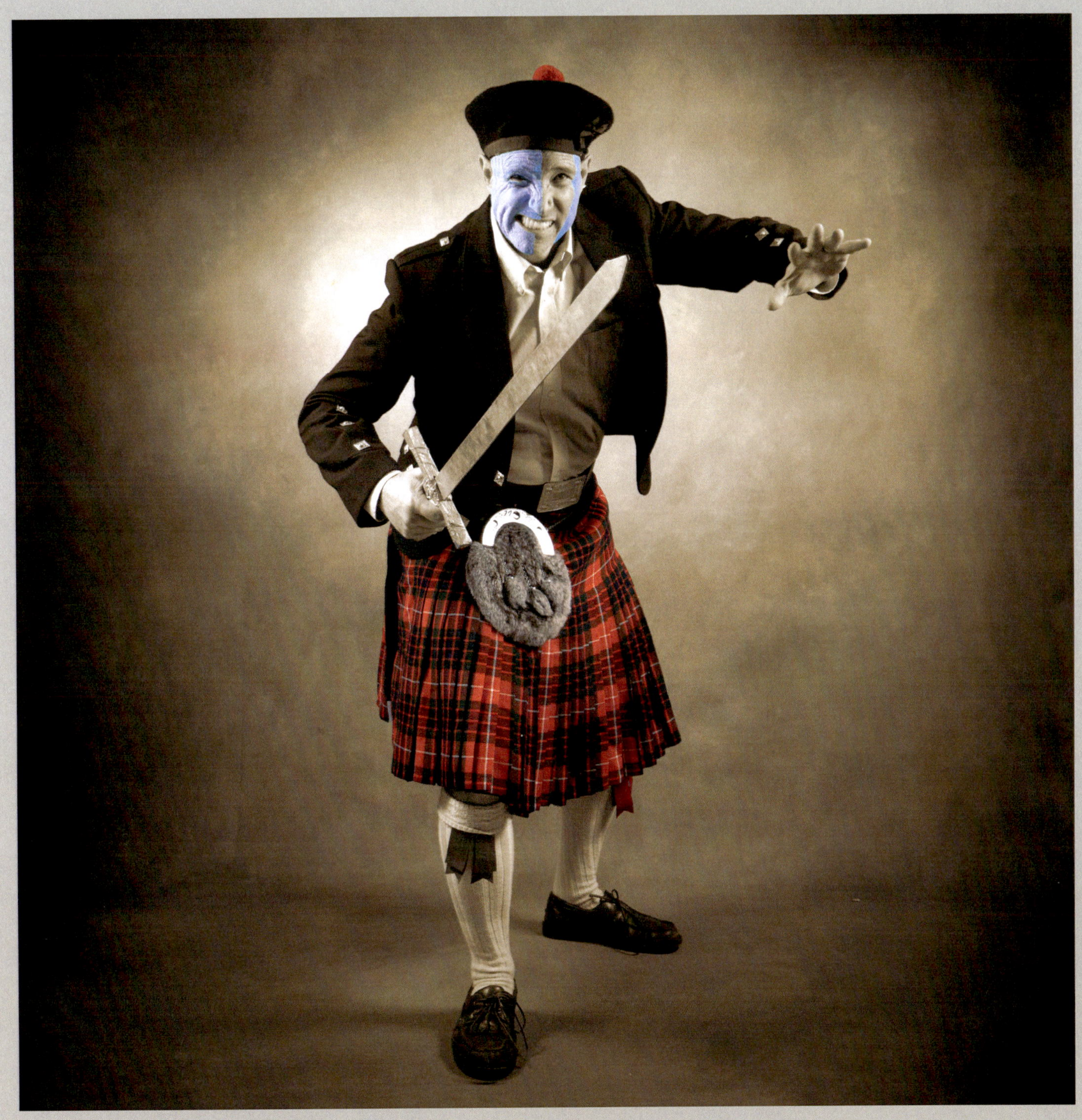

Don Frazier, *History Teacher.* -
"KILT, It's what happened to the last person who called it a skirt."

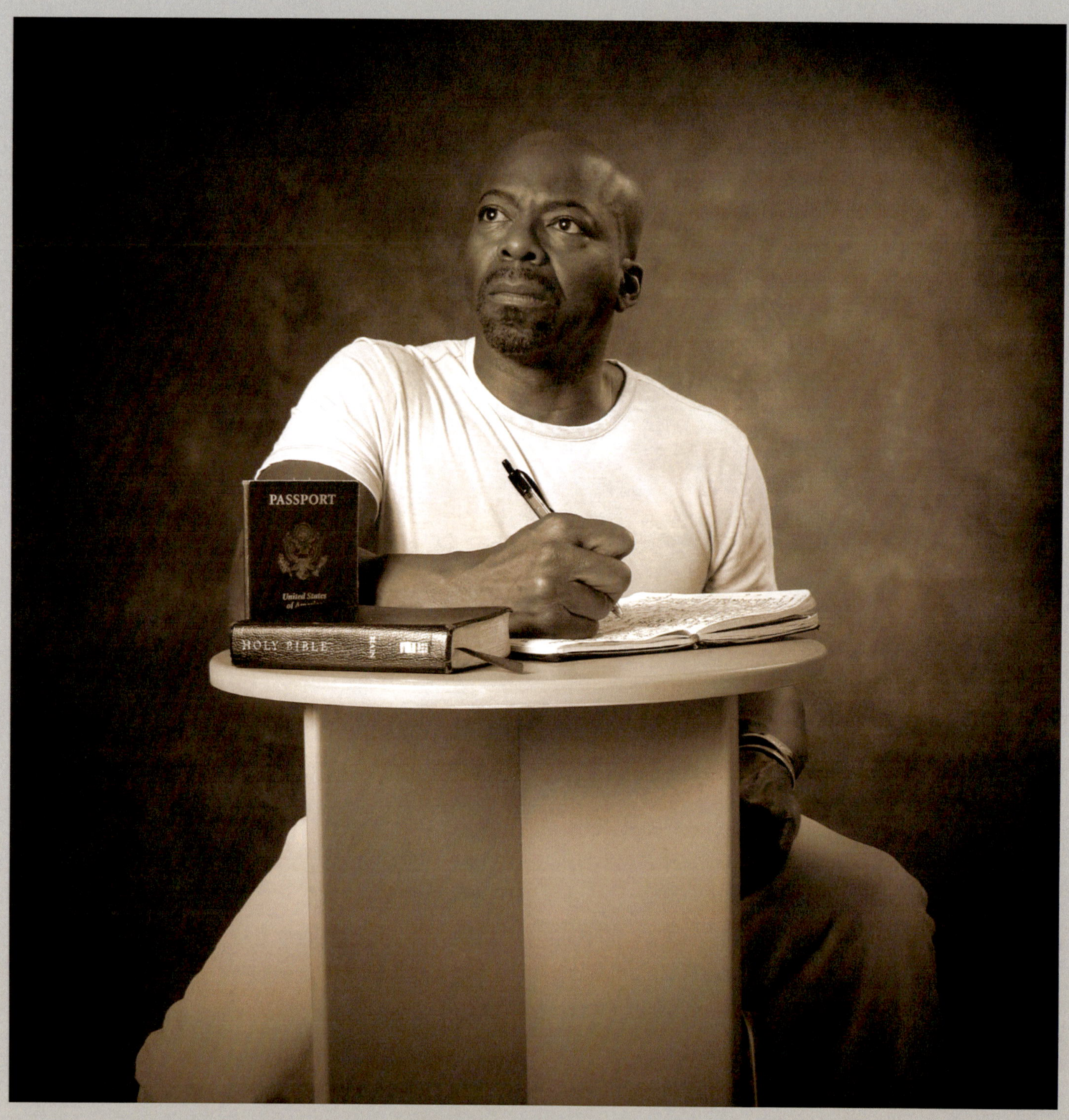

Jazz Thompson, *Spanish & French Language Teacher.* -
"For me to live is Christ and to die is gain." - Philippians 1:21

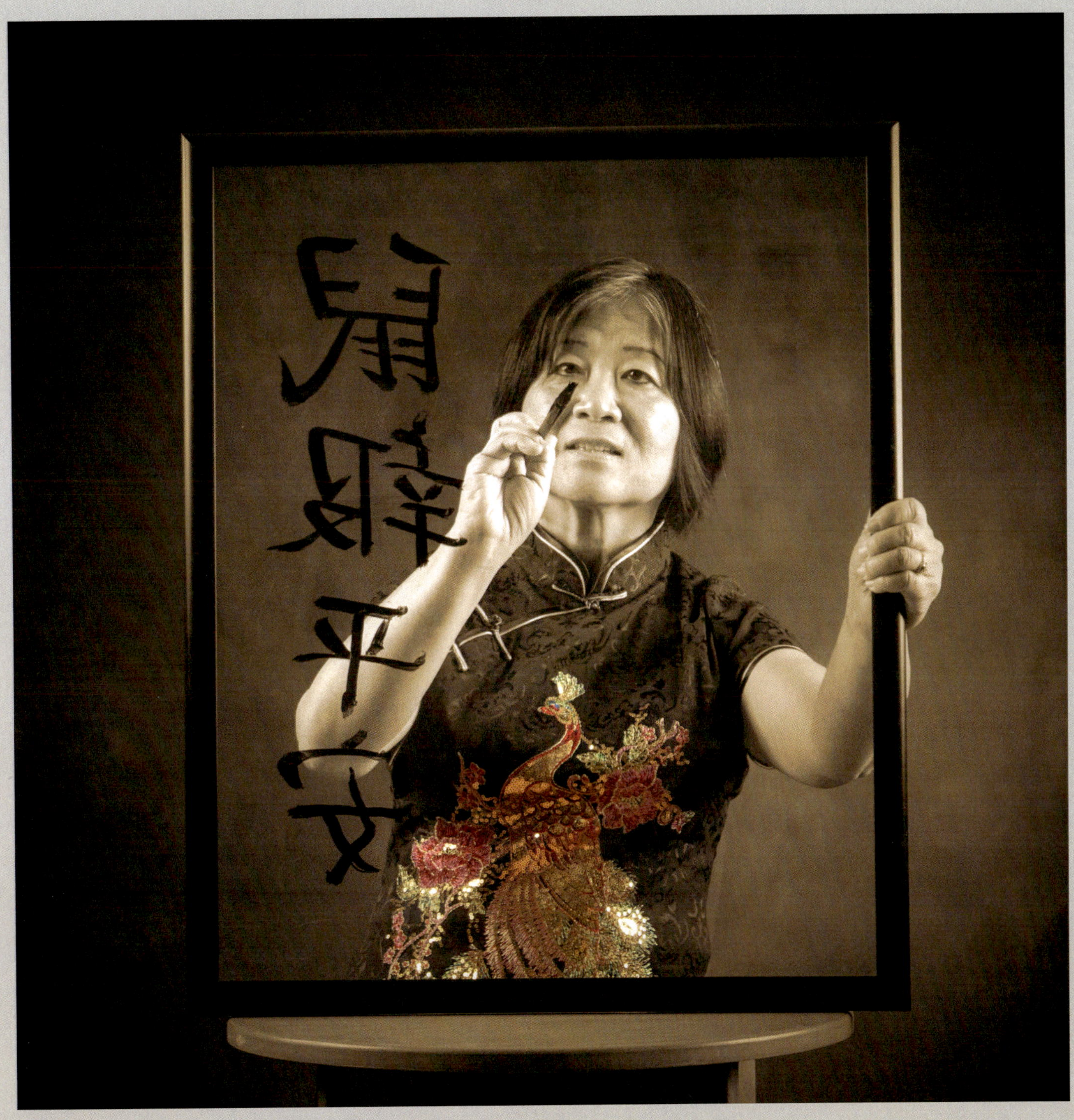

Grace Anderson, *Chinese Language Teacher.* -
"Being a teacher has been my passion since the 3rd grade. I enjoy teaching and learning each day."

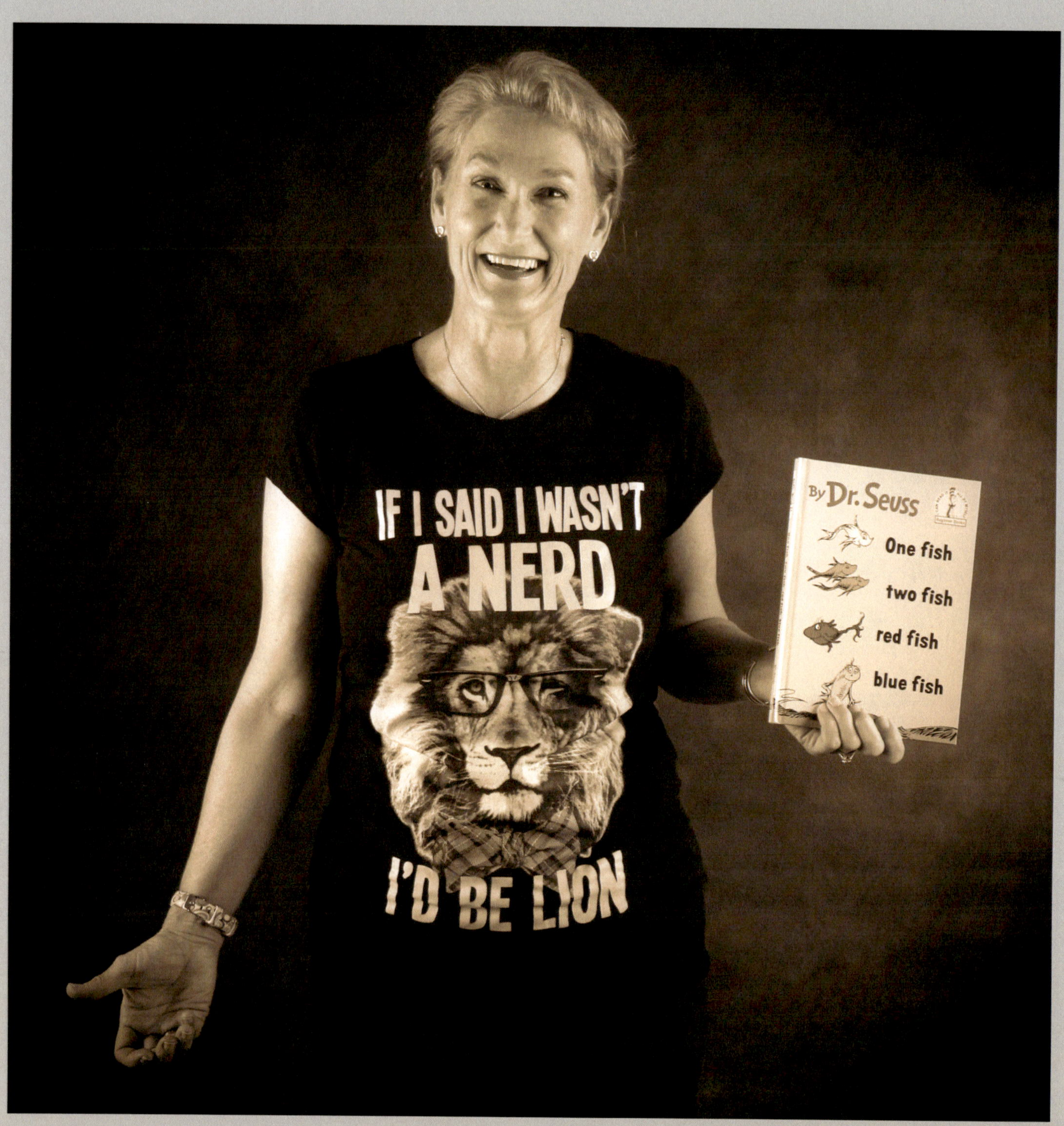

Jackie Payne, *Math Teacher.*

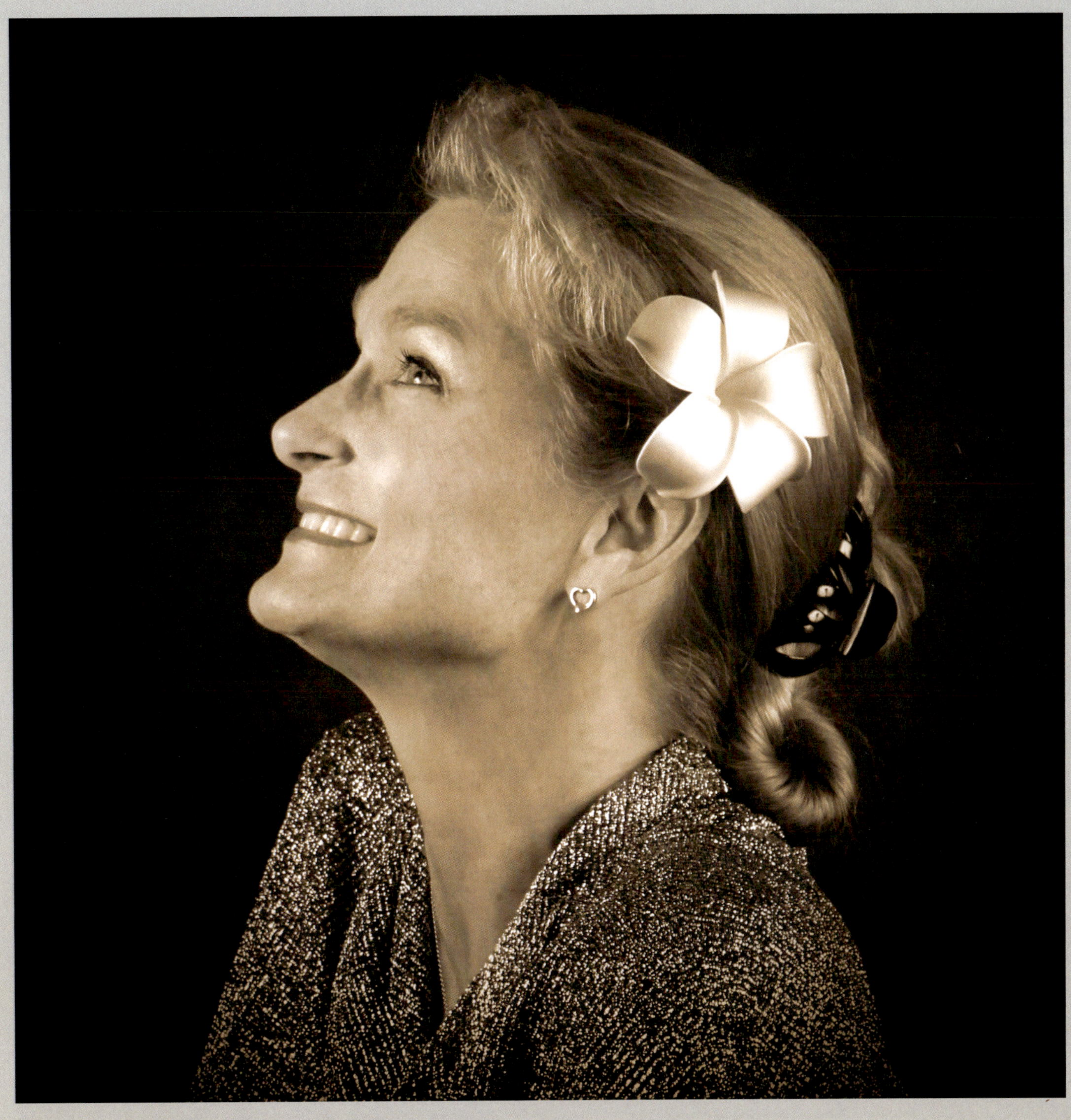

Jackie Payne, *Math Teacher.* -
"He 'olina leo ka ke aloha" which means "There is joy in the voice of love."

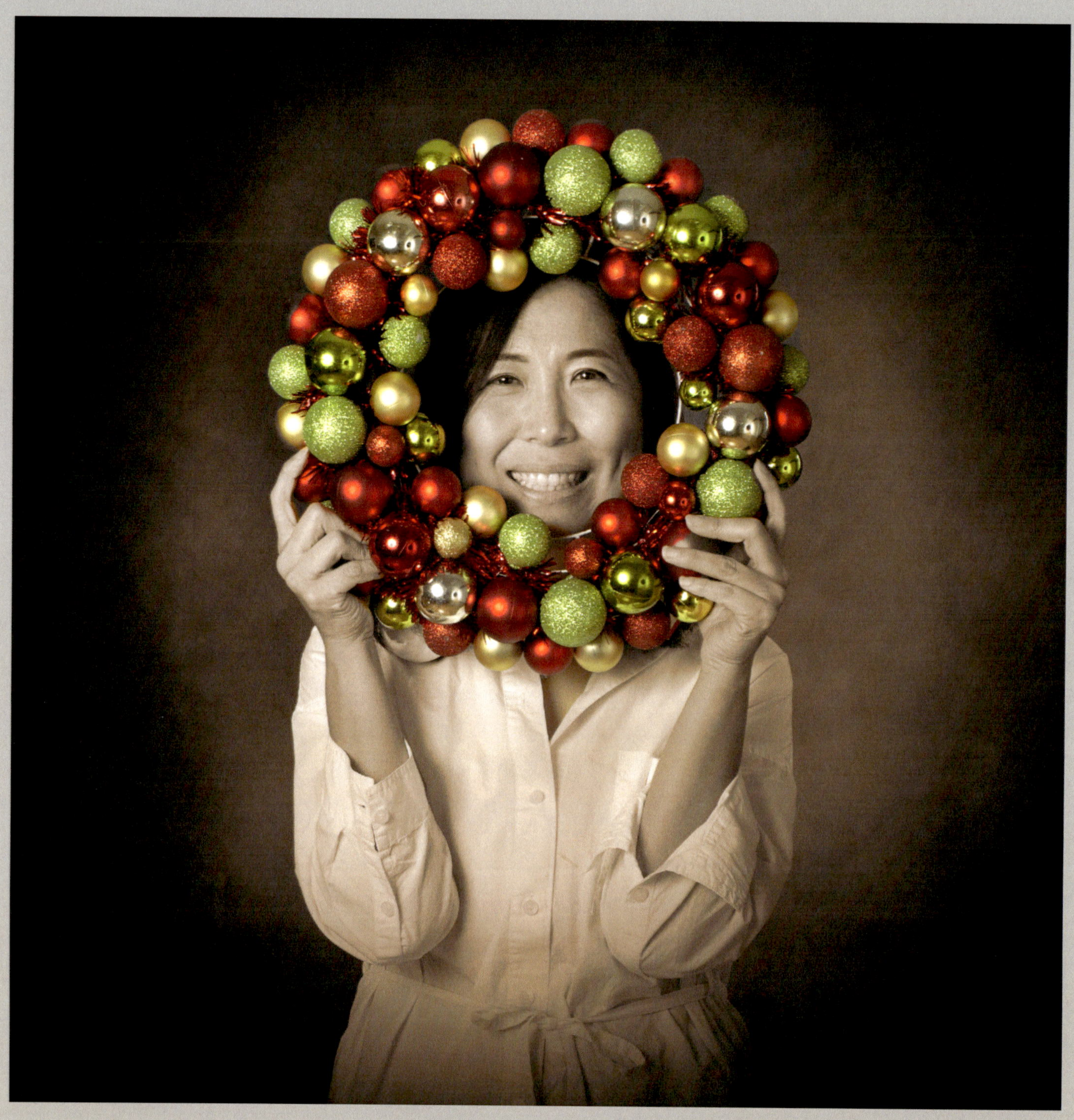

June Choi, *Korean Language Teacher.* -
"Christmas isn't just a day, it's a frame of mind." - Valentine Davies

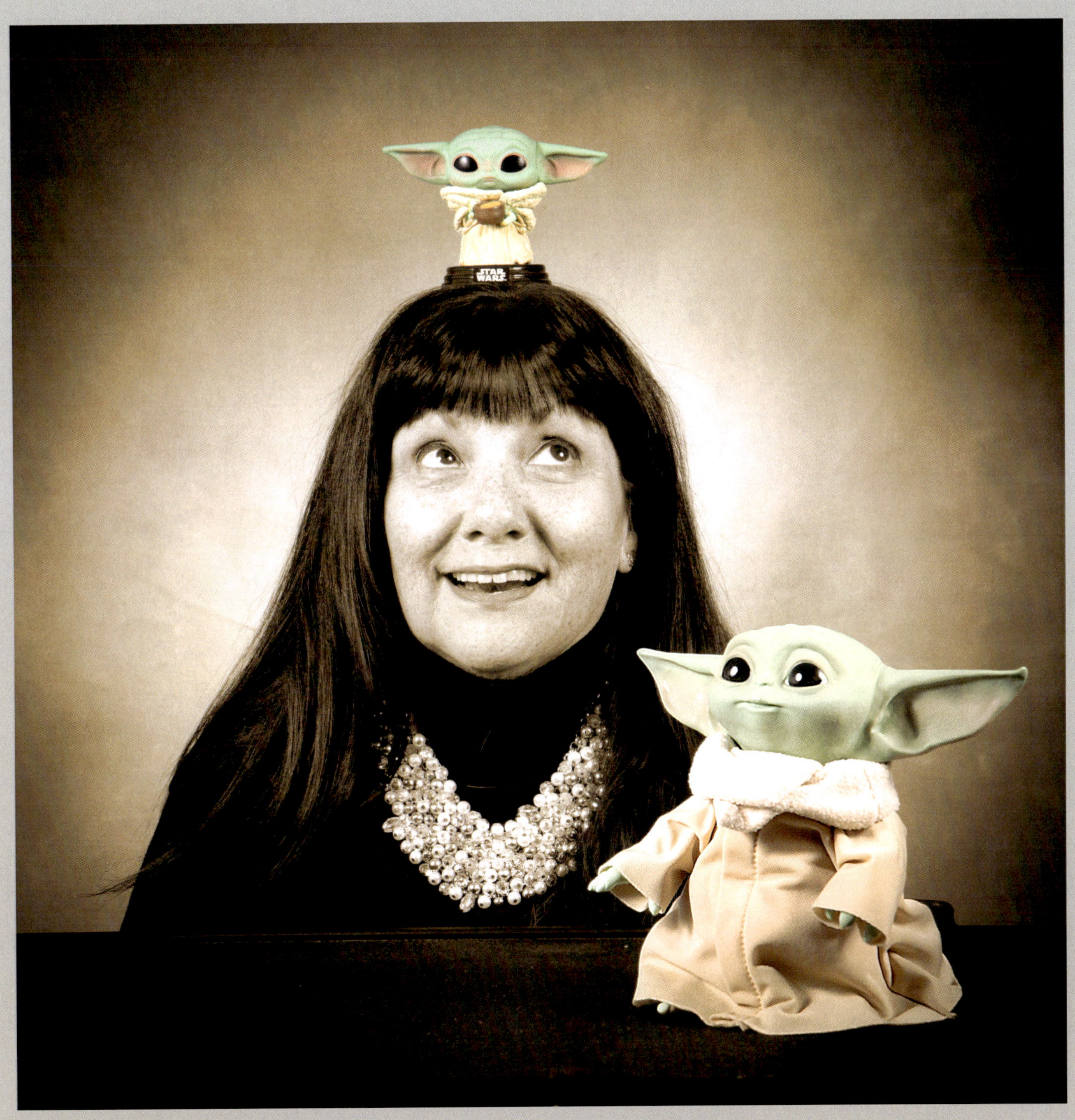

Gloria Juge, *Counseling Staff.* -
"Slow down. Build moments that carry your legacy."

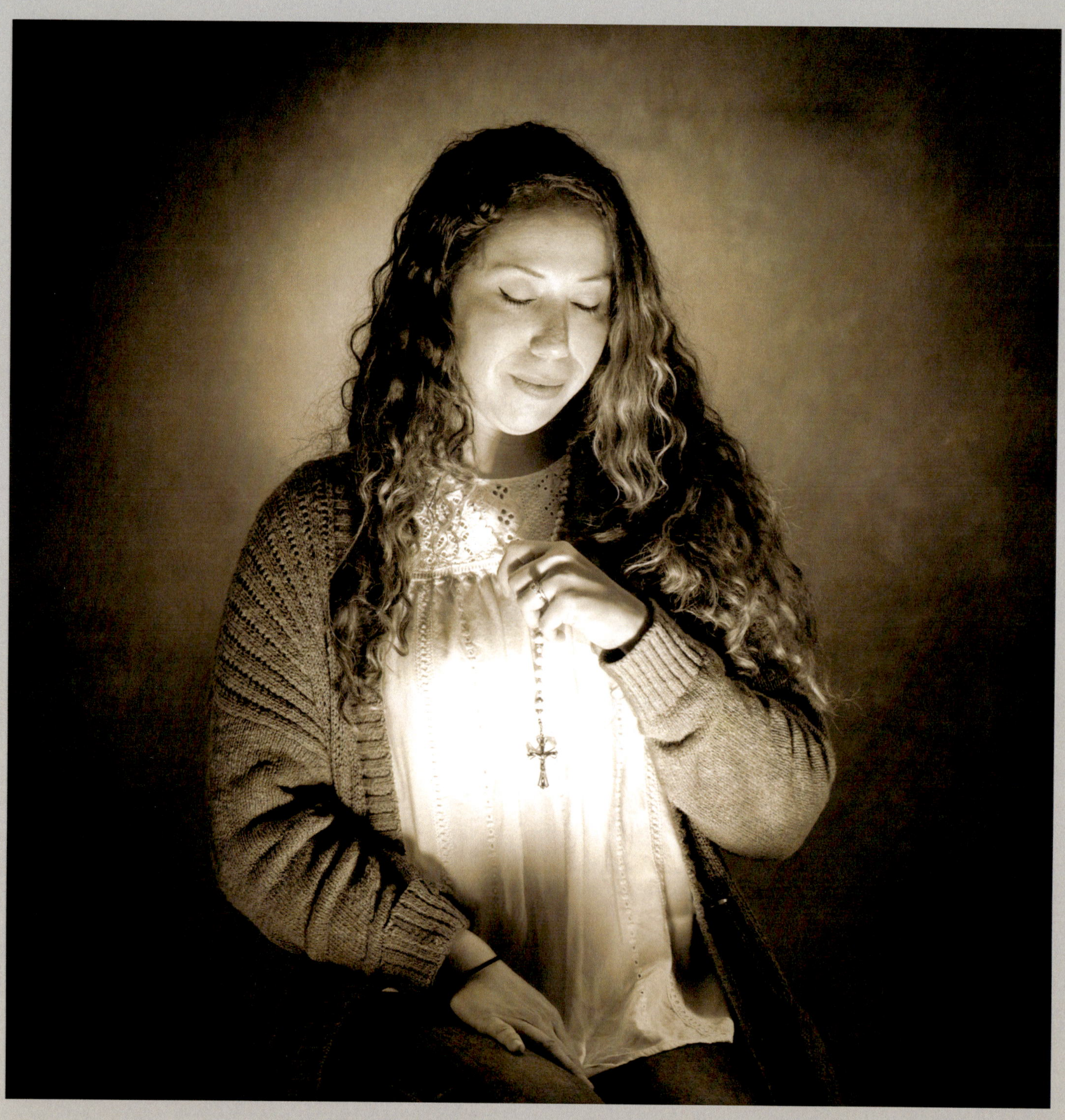

Katherine Angell, *School Psychologist, Soleado Elementary.* -
"Where there is hatred, let me sow love. Where there is injury, pardon. Where there is doubt, faith." - Saint Francis of Assisi

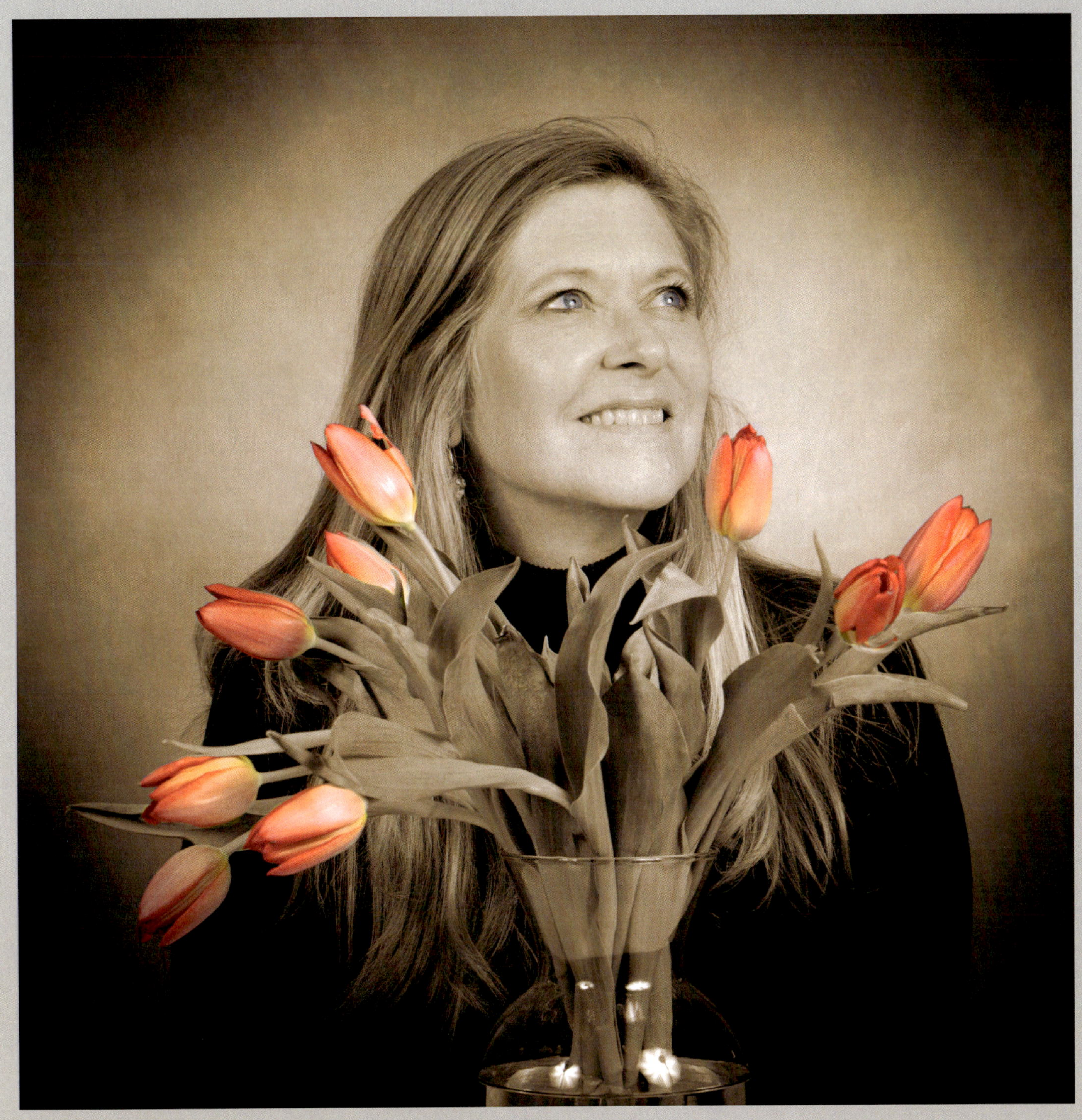

Lisa Turner, *Soleado Elementary Teacher.* -
"One day you will look back and see all along you were blooming."

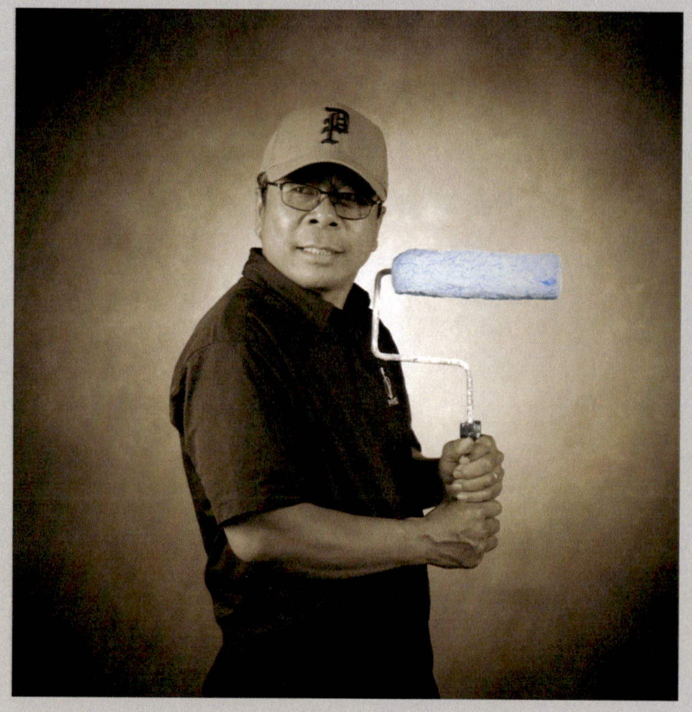

Sobin Neung, *Custodian.*

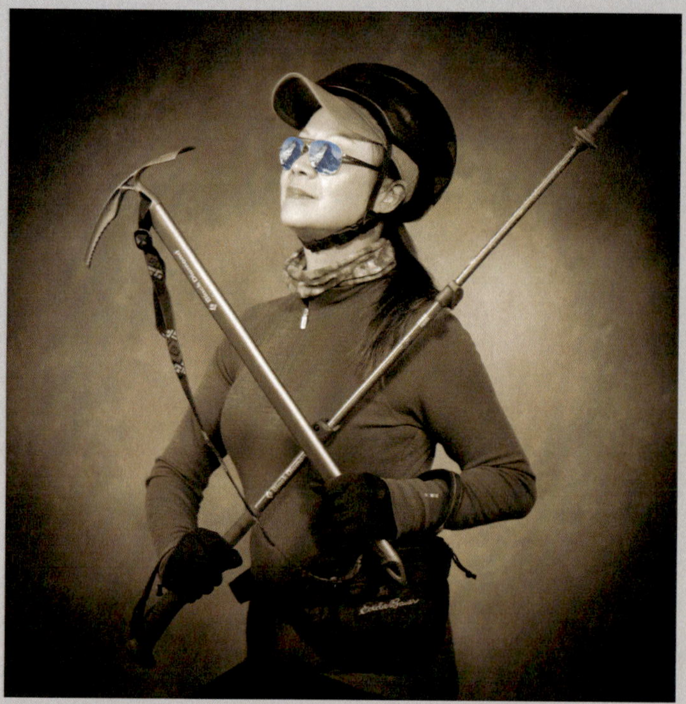

Curie Fleder, *Study Skills Teacher.* -
"If you wanna do something, you'll find
a way; if you don't wanna do something,
you'll find an excuse."

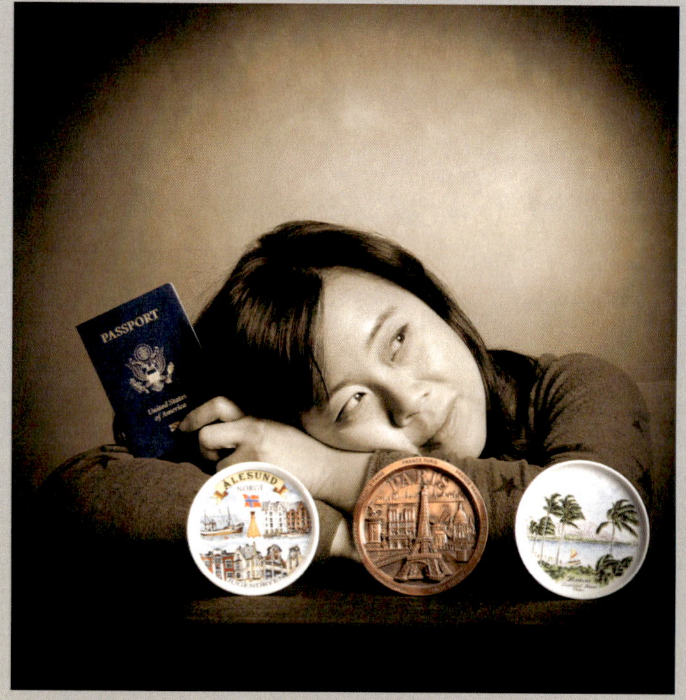

Emily Chen, *Geometry & Algebra Teacher.* -
"There was nowhere to go but everywhere,
so just keep rolling under the stars." - Jack
Kerouac

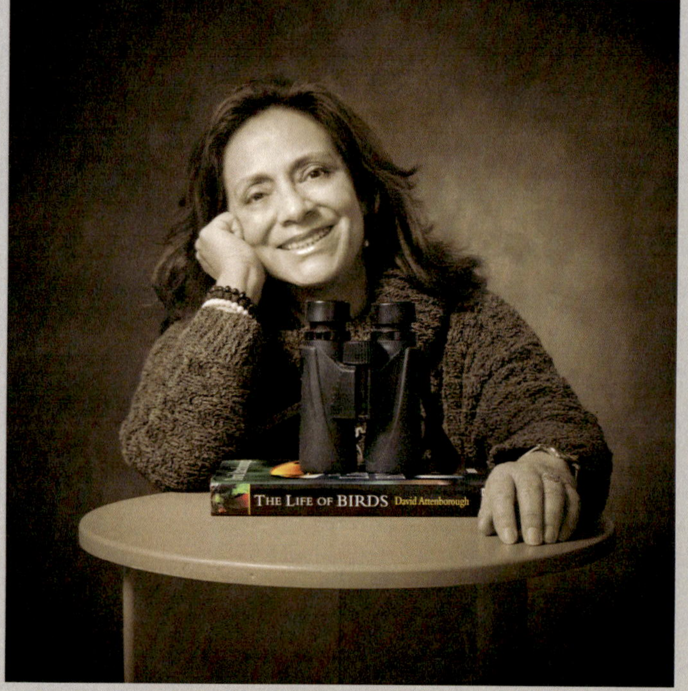

Josefina Madunich, *Spanish Language
Teacher.* -
"Happiness is to do what you have passion
for, and make a living with it."

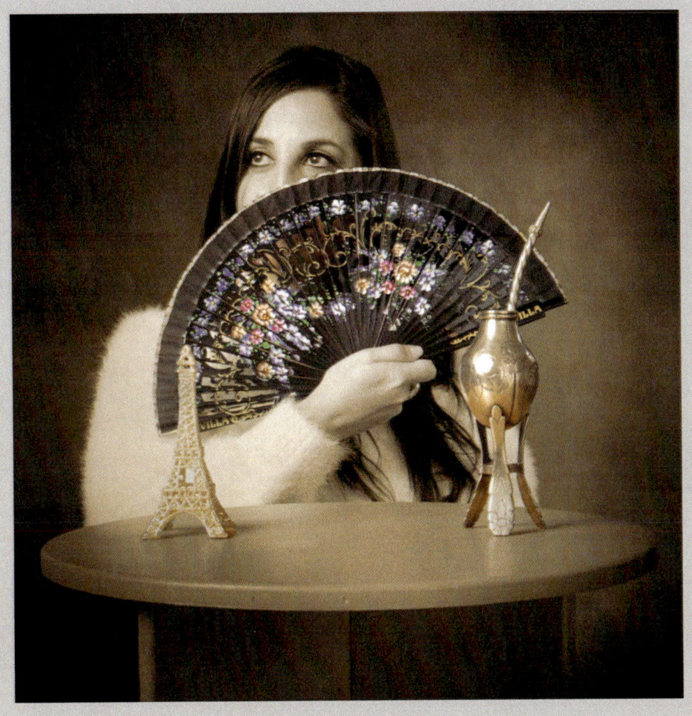

Jacqueline Valerio, *Spanish Language Teacher.*

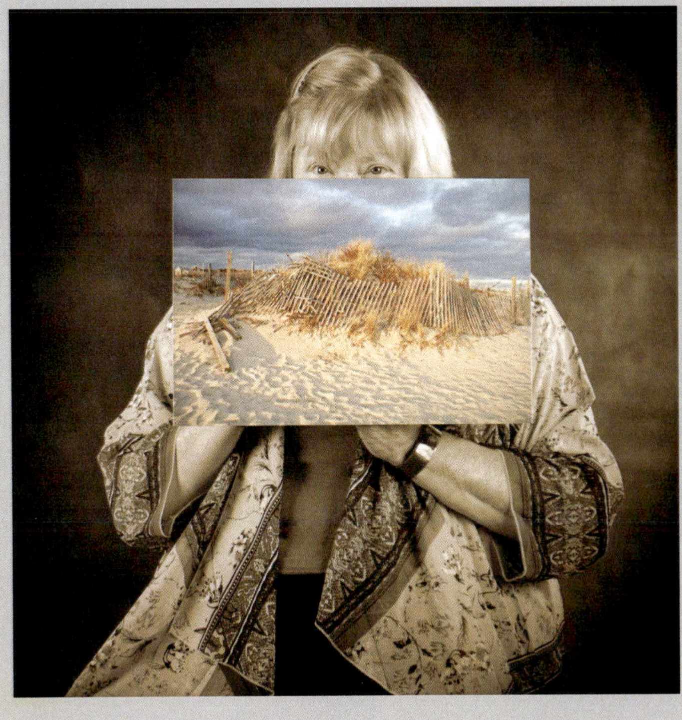

Bonnie Kielbach, *Attendance Head.* - "There's no place like home if only in my dreams."

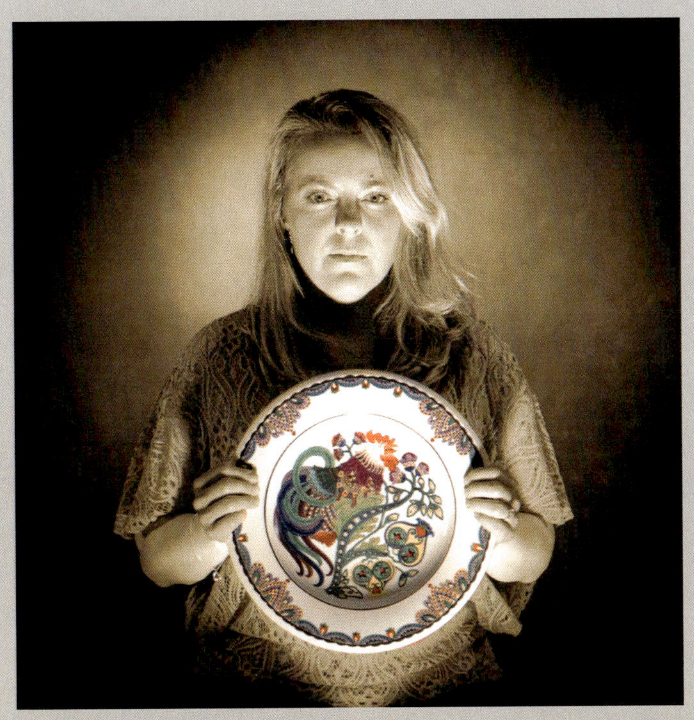

Jana Smith, *Soleado Elementary Teacher.*

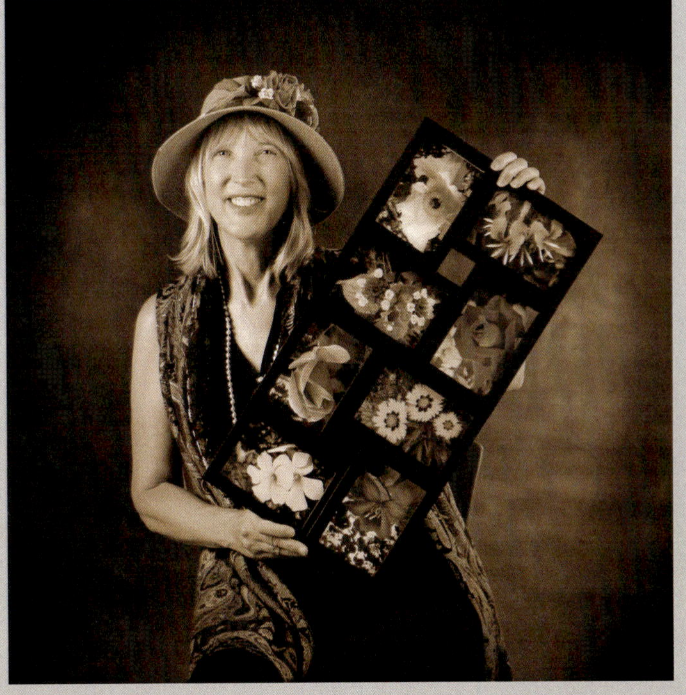

Bonnie Angle, *Speech Therapist.* - "May flowers always line your path and sunshine light your day. May songbirds serenade you every step along the way." - Irish Blessing

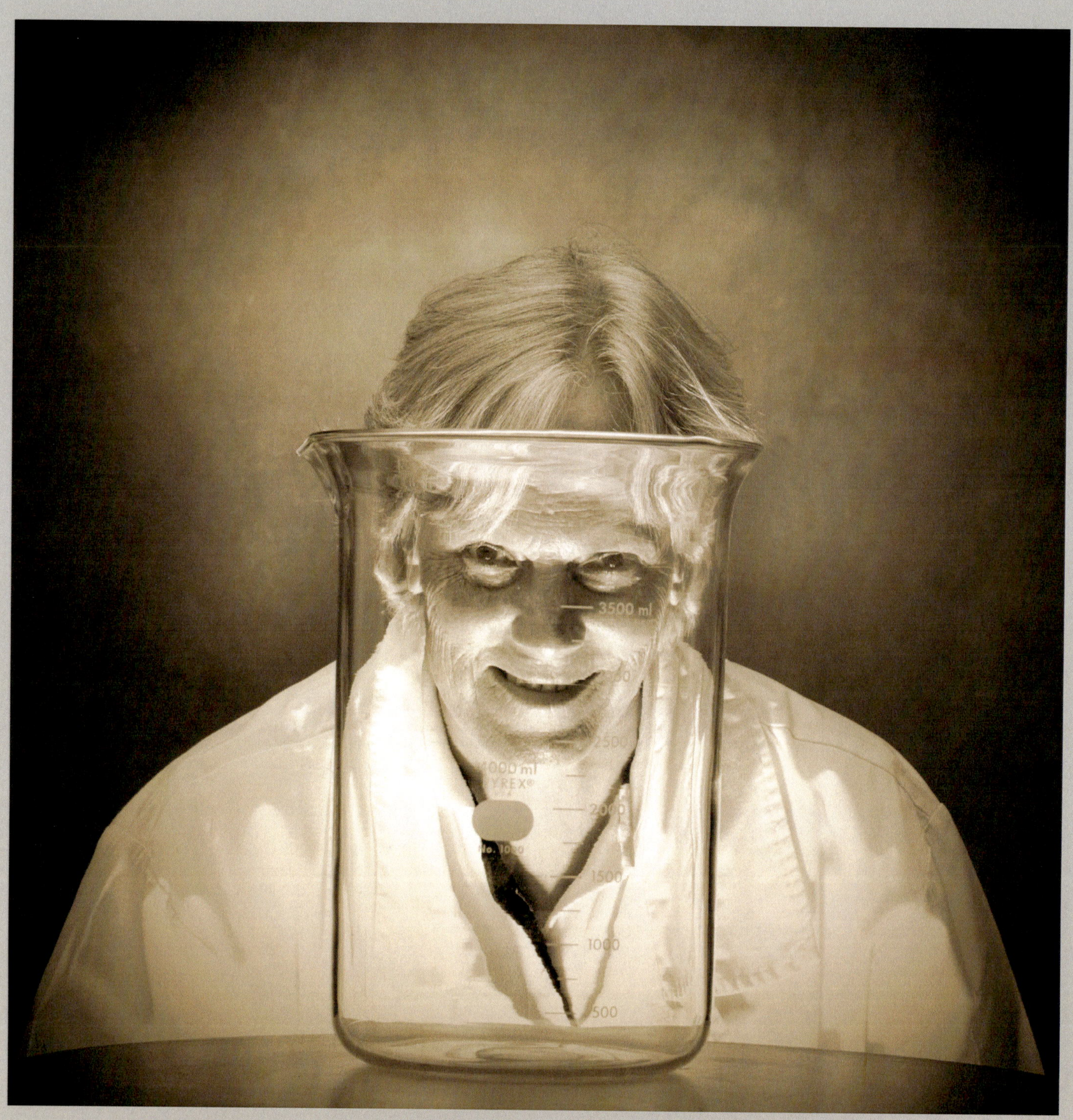

Paula Borstel, *Chemistry Teacher.*

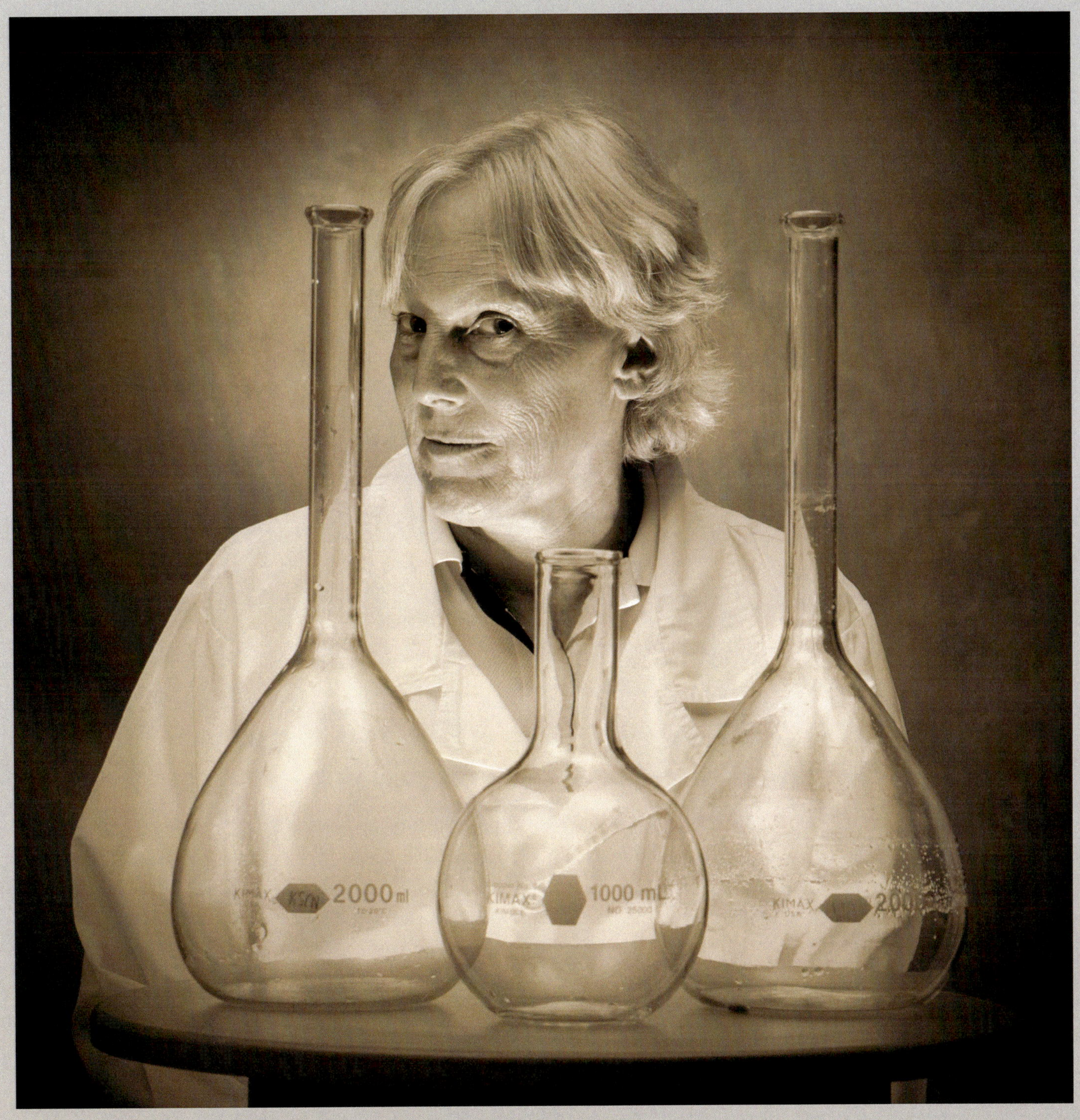

Paula Borstel, *Chemistry Teacher.* -
"My emails are sent with recycled electrons and biodegradable photons: Save the Earth, it is the only planet with chocolate!"

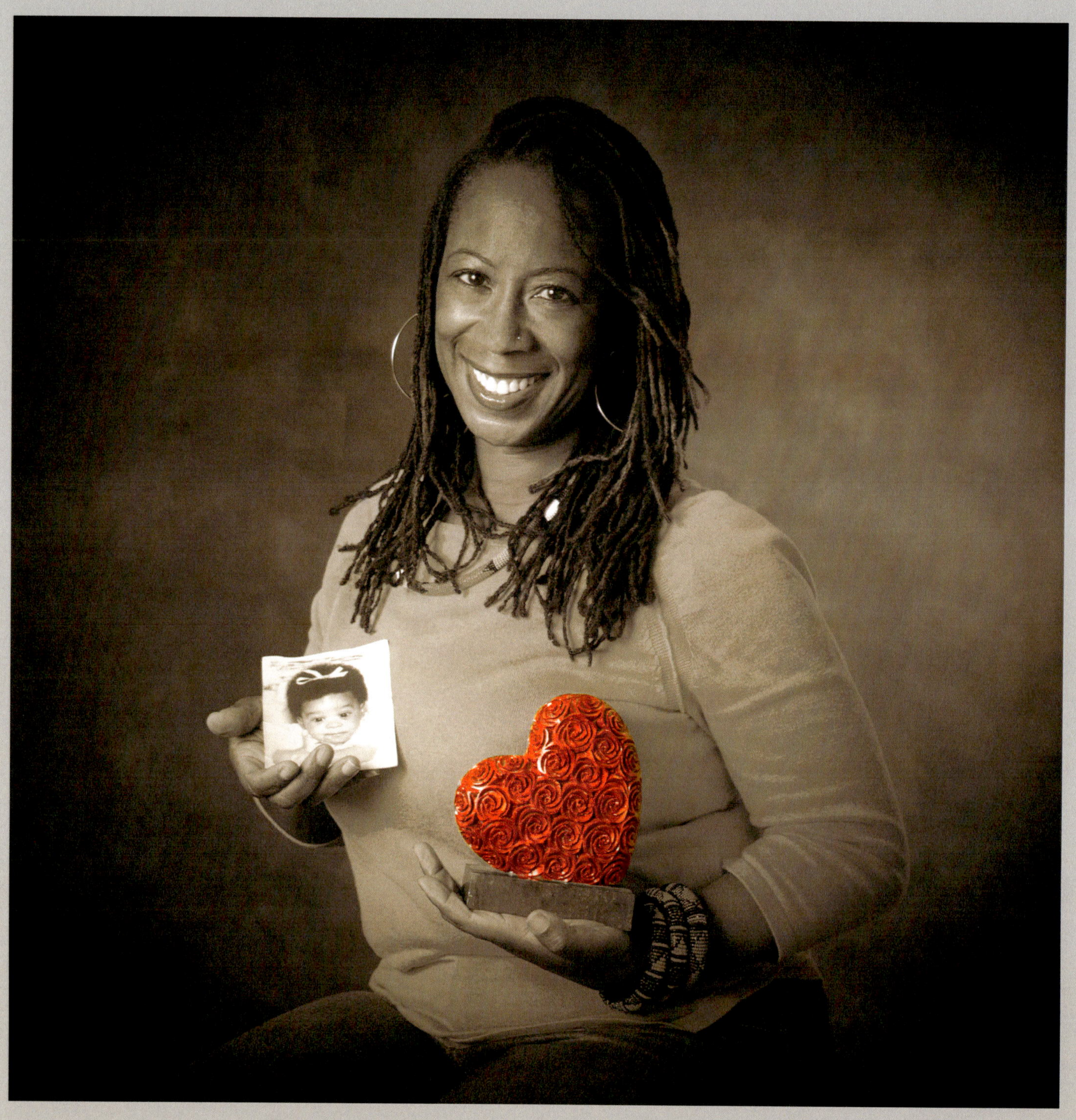

Kisha Williams, *SPED Cliairperson.* -
"Spread love everywhere you go. Let no one ever come to you without leaving happier." -
Mother Teresa

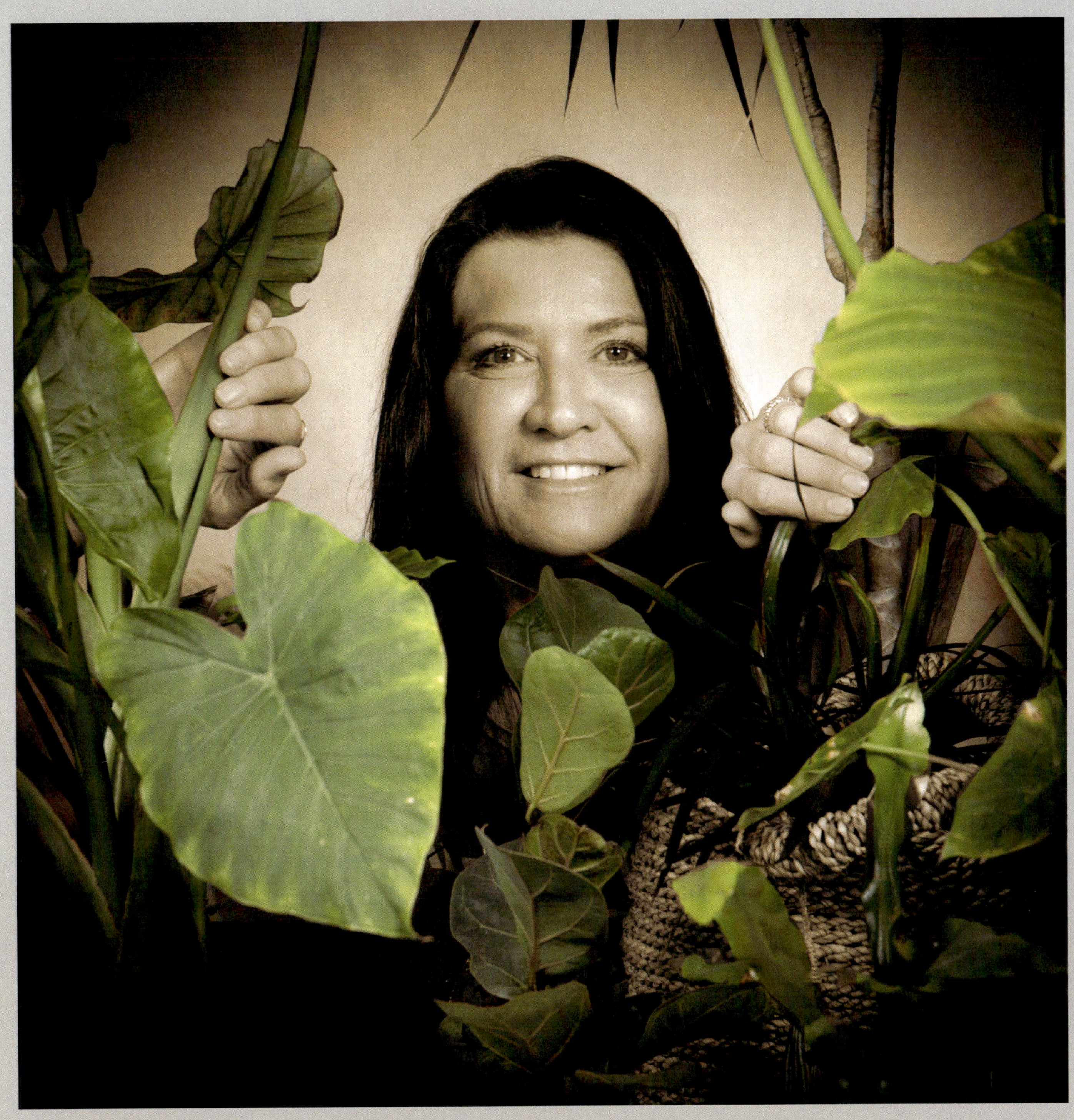

Shannon Bogart, *Soleado Elementary Teacher.* -
"Never underestimate the power of a planted seed."

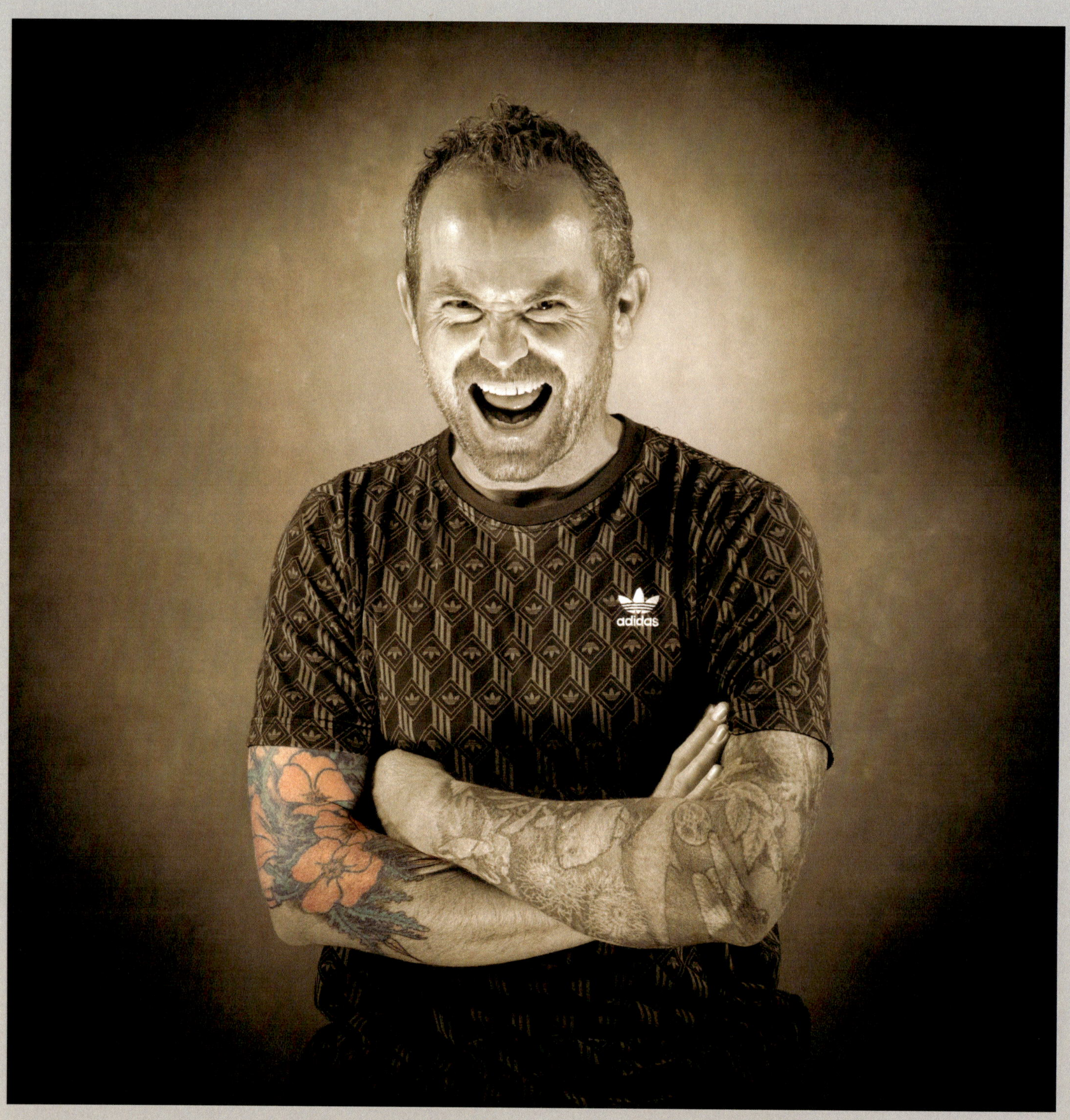

Patrick Daley, *Soccer Coach.* -
"Embrace your passions, ink your values, and spread the joy of learning. Happiness is the key that unlocks a fulfilling life."

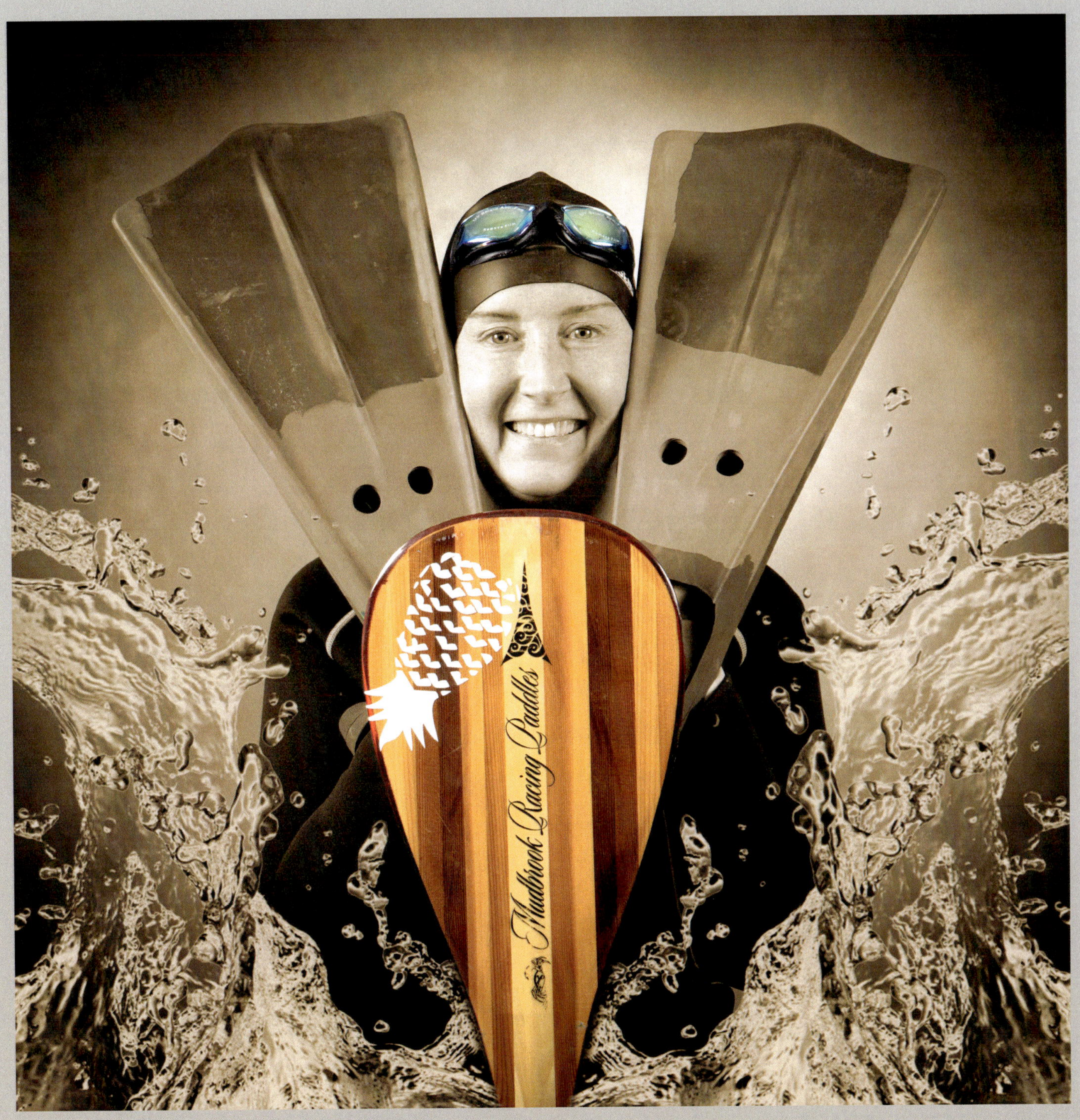

Lisa Dohren, *English Teacher.* -
"98% of what a butterfly does is irrelevant, allegedly."

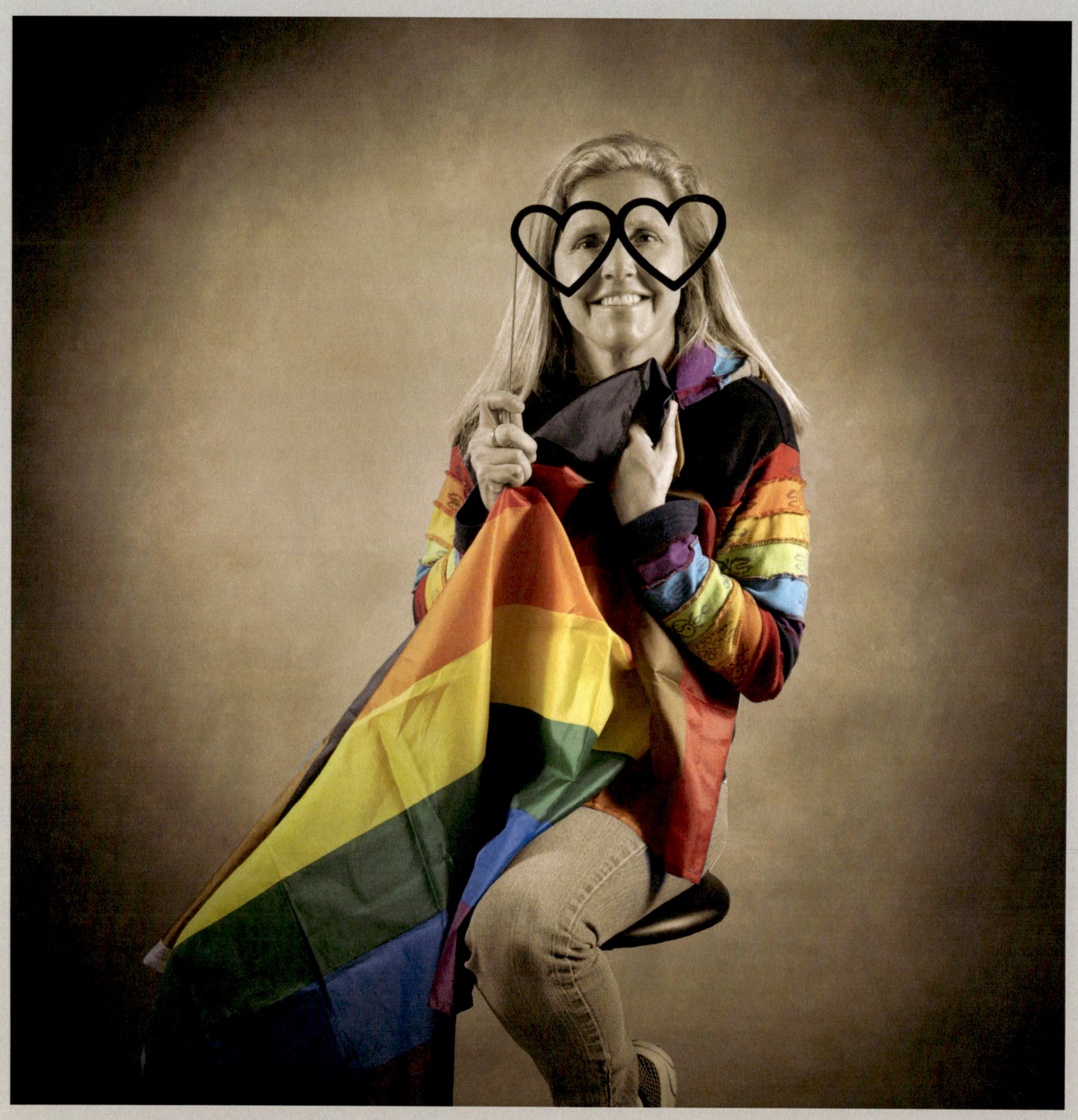

Mariana Donahoe, *Spanish Language Teacher.* -
"We must always take sides. Neutrality helps the oppressor, never the victim. Silence
encourages the tormentor, never the tormented. Sometimes we must interfere."

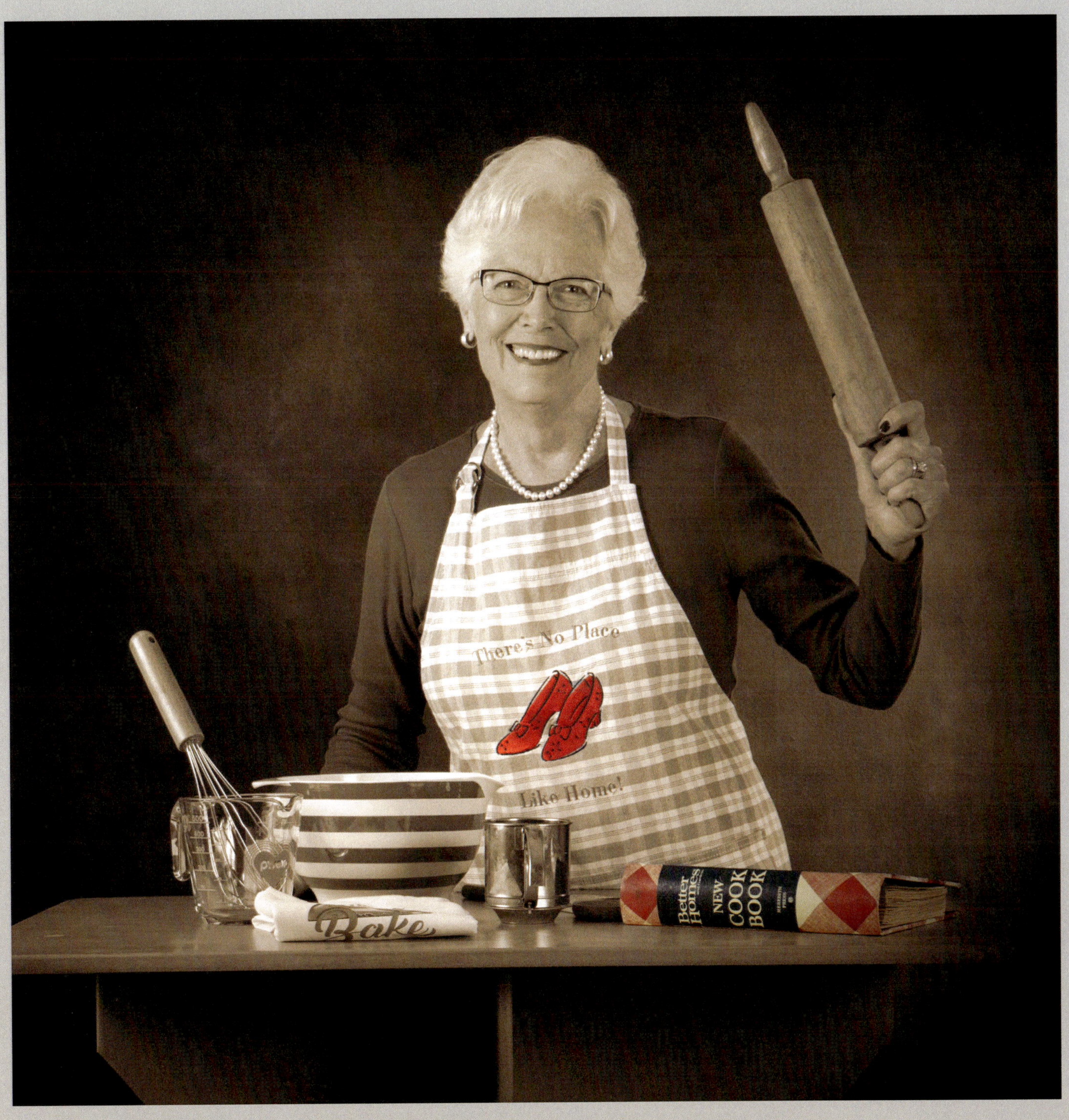

Margaret Benson, *Secretary.* -
"Today you WILL enjoy the good things in life. Just roll with it."

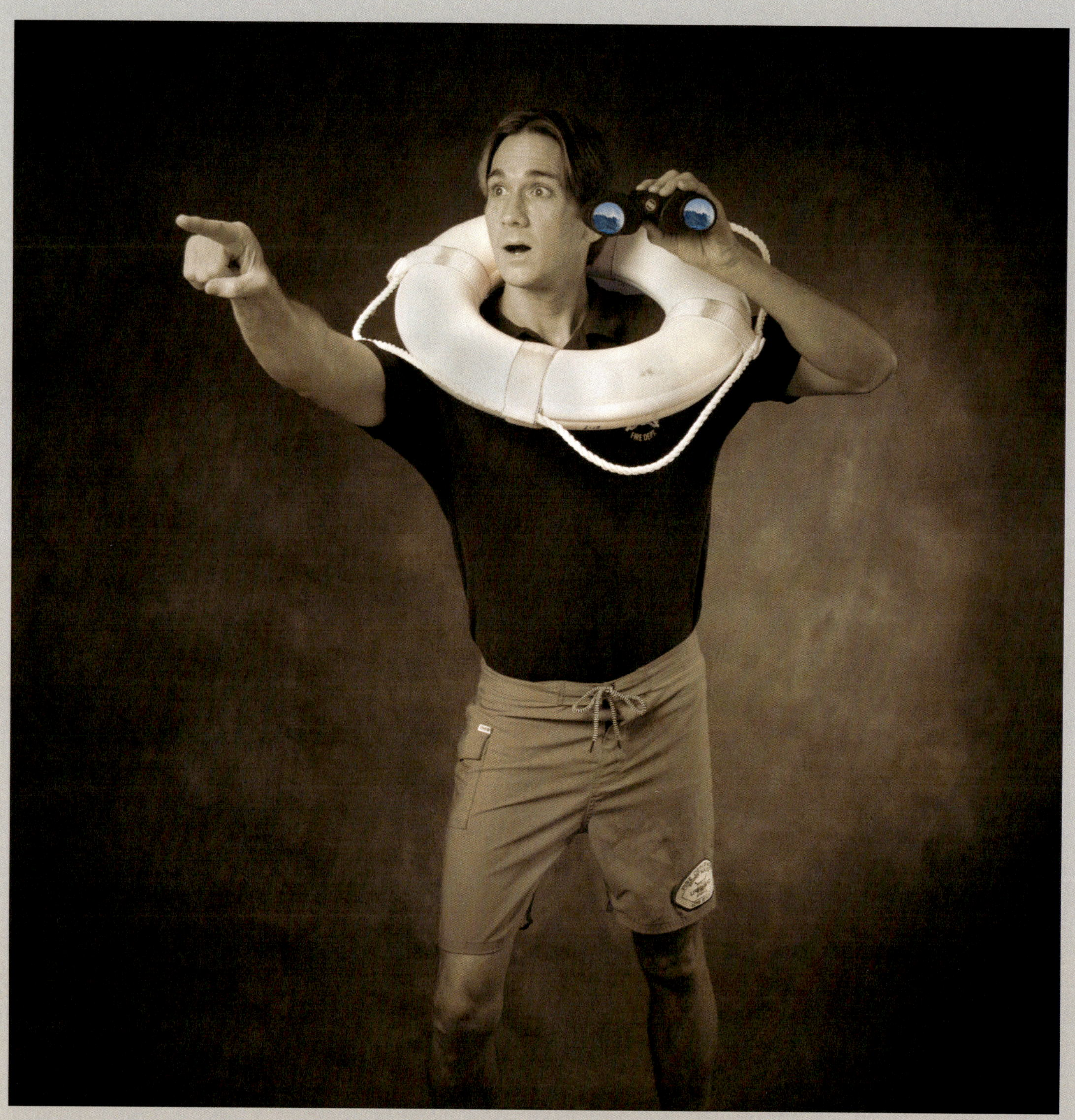

Michael Wanmer, *Associate Principal.*

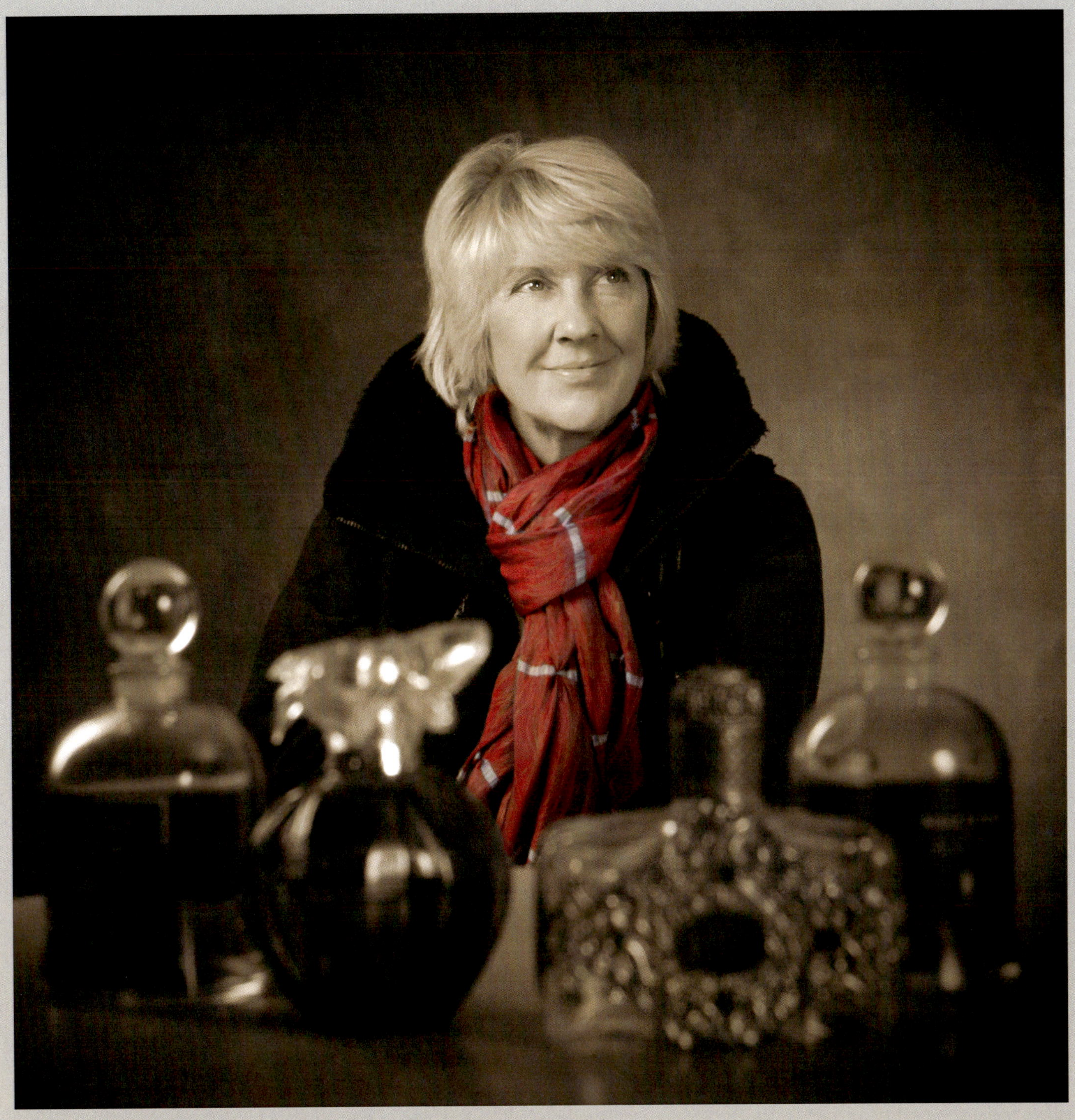

Marie France Sam, *French Language Teacher.* -
"If you want to build a ship, don't drum up people to collect wood and don't assign them
tasks and work, but rather teach them to long for the endless immensity of the sea." -
Antoine de Saint-Exupery

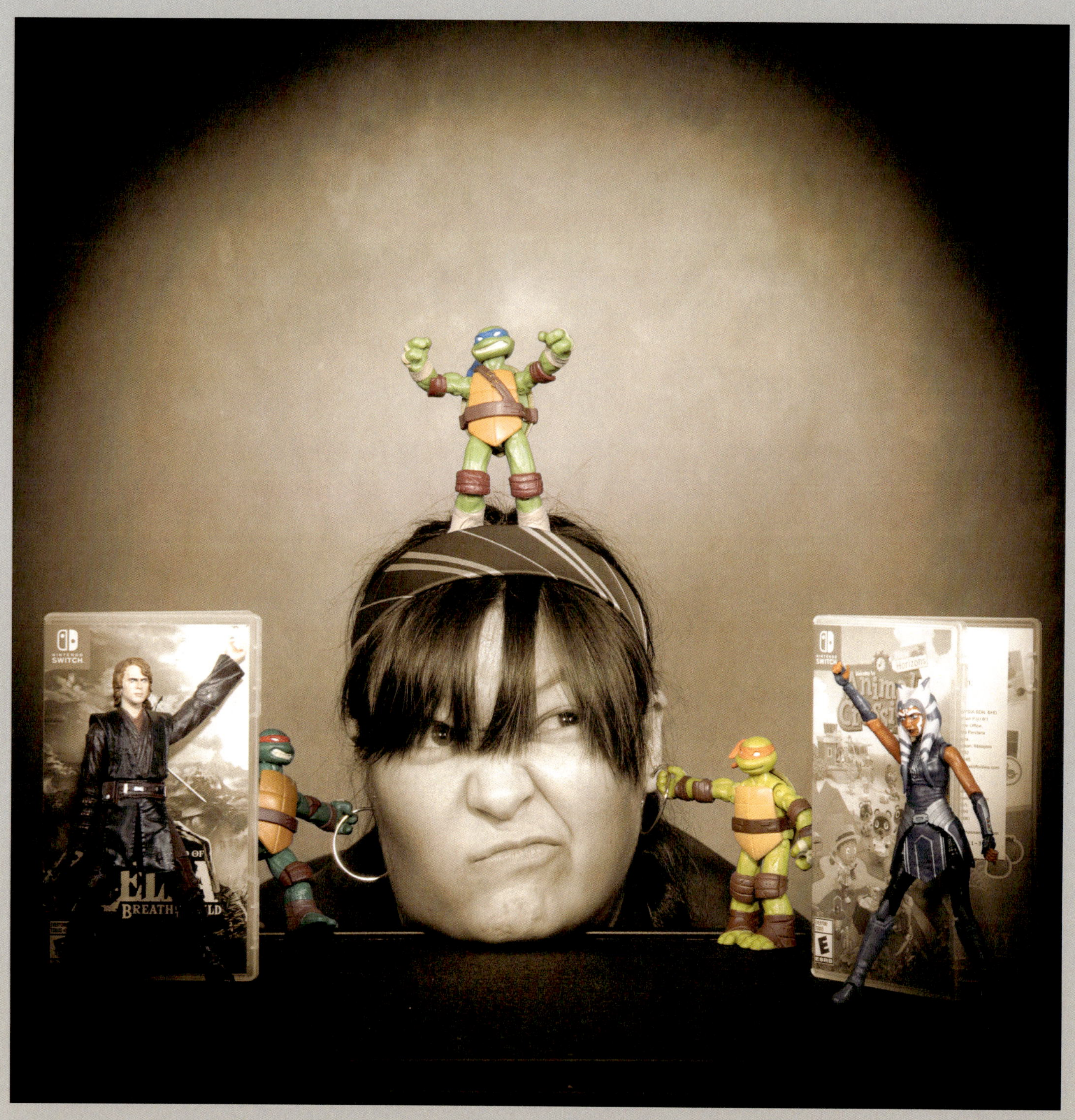

Michelle Smith, *Geometry Teacher.* -
"When I became a man I put away childish things, including the fear of childishness and the desire to be very grown up." - C. S. Lewis

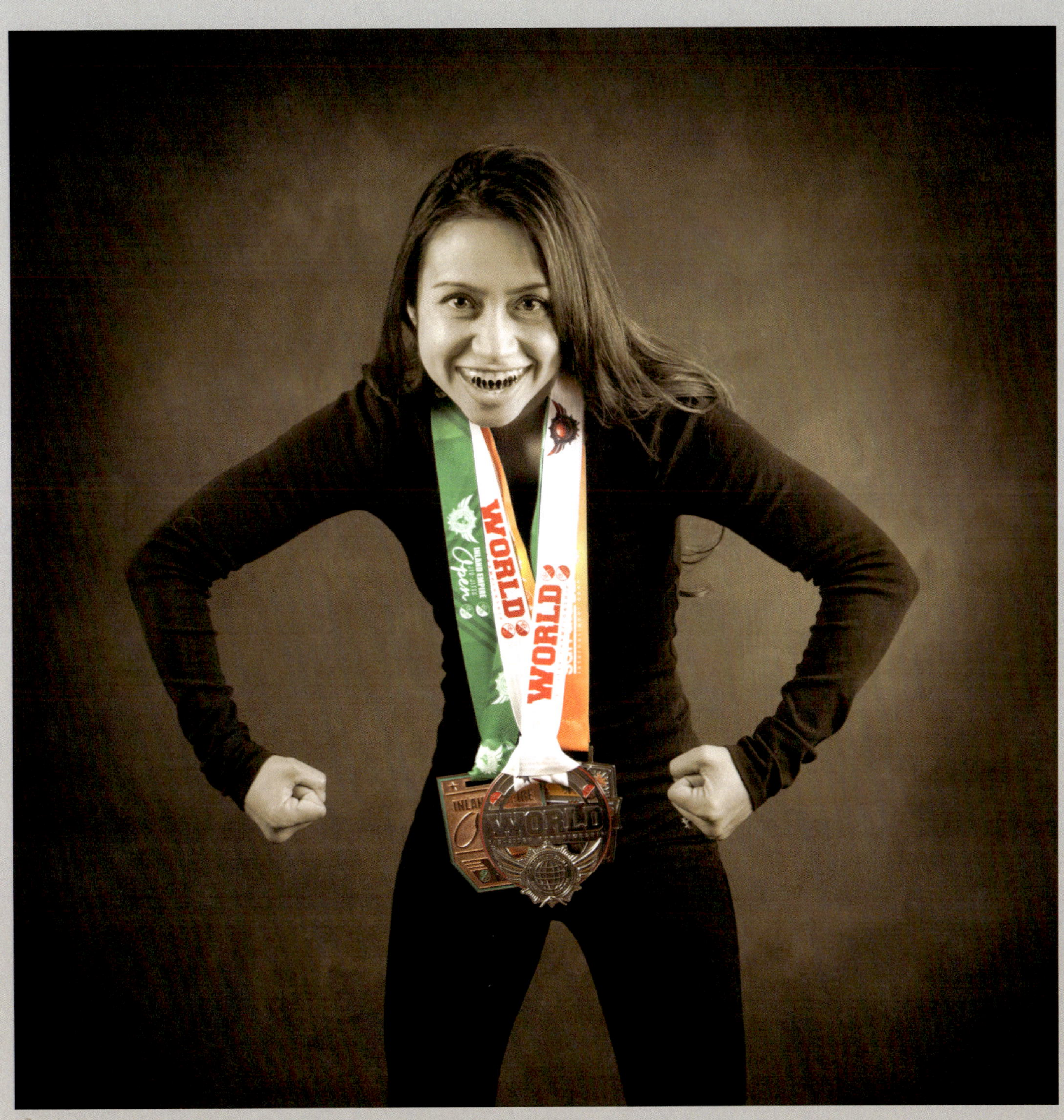

Melissa Meeks, *Student Aide.*

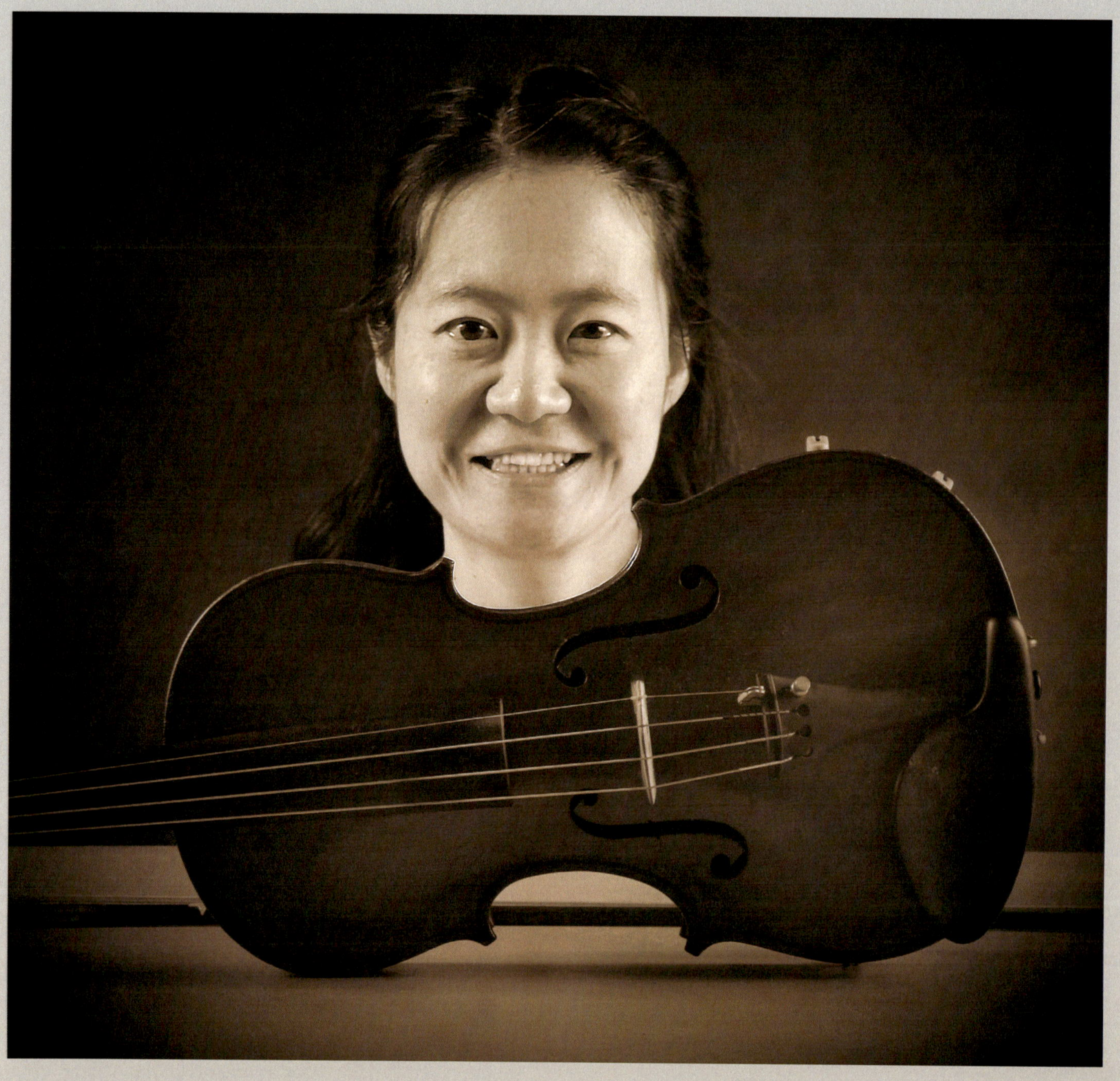

Michiko Yu, *Japanese Language Teacher.* -
"Everything has beauty, but not everyone sees it." - Confucius

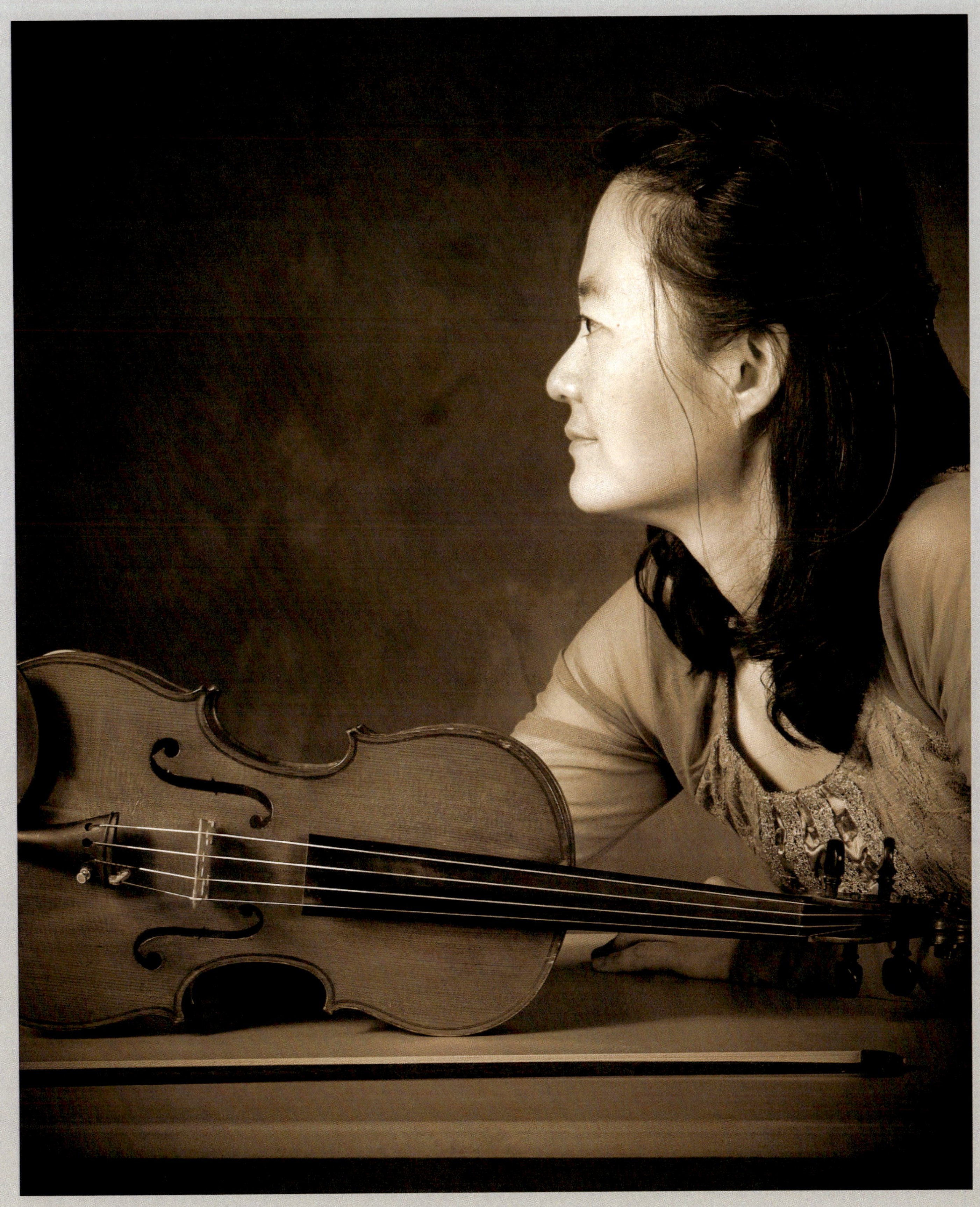

Michiko Yu, *Japanese Language Teacher.*

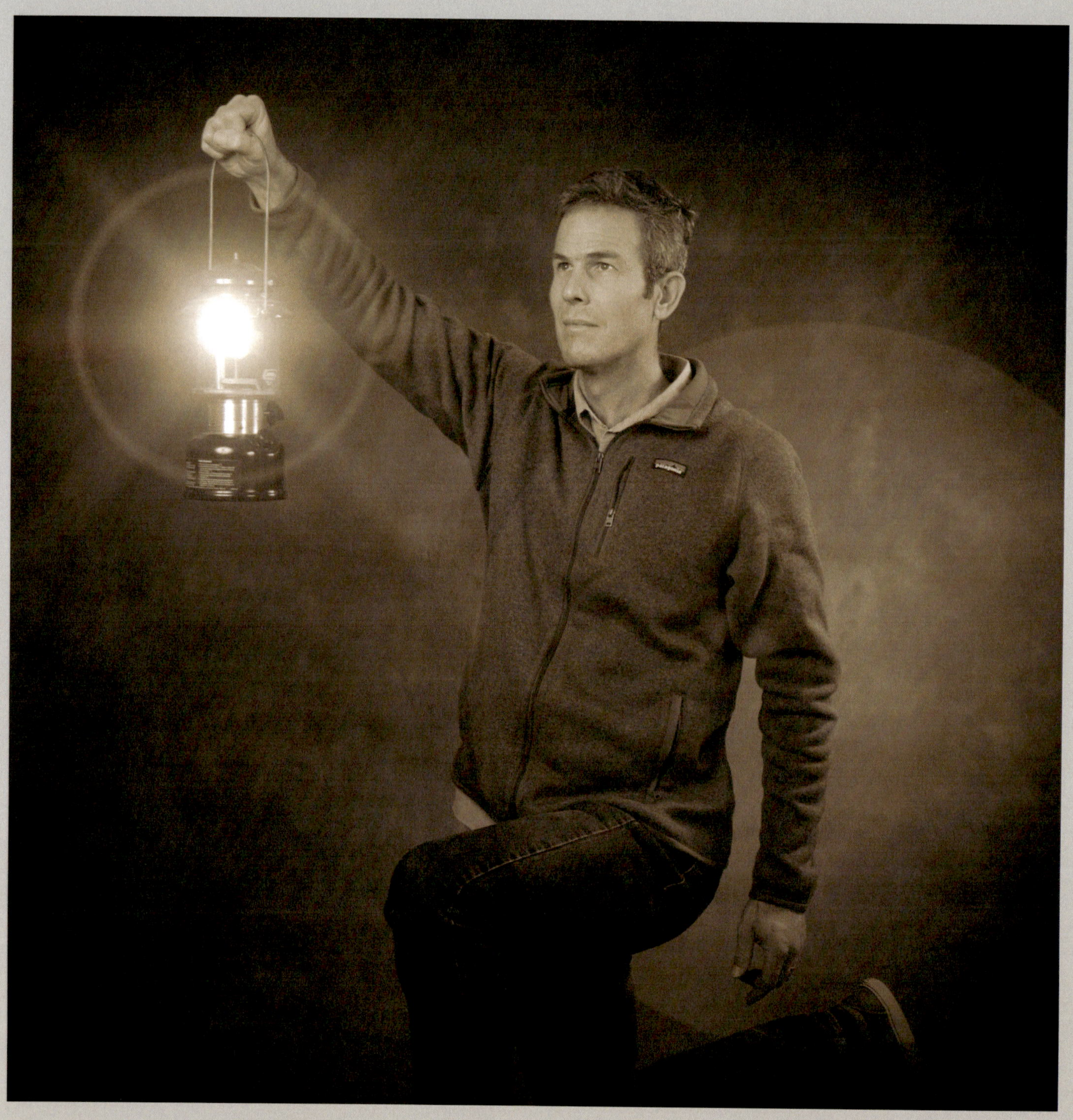

Mike Spaulding, *AP Physics & AVID Teacher.* -
"Be the change you want to see in the world." - Mahatma Gandhi

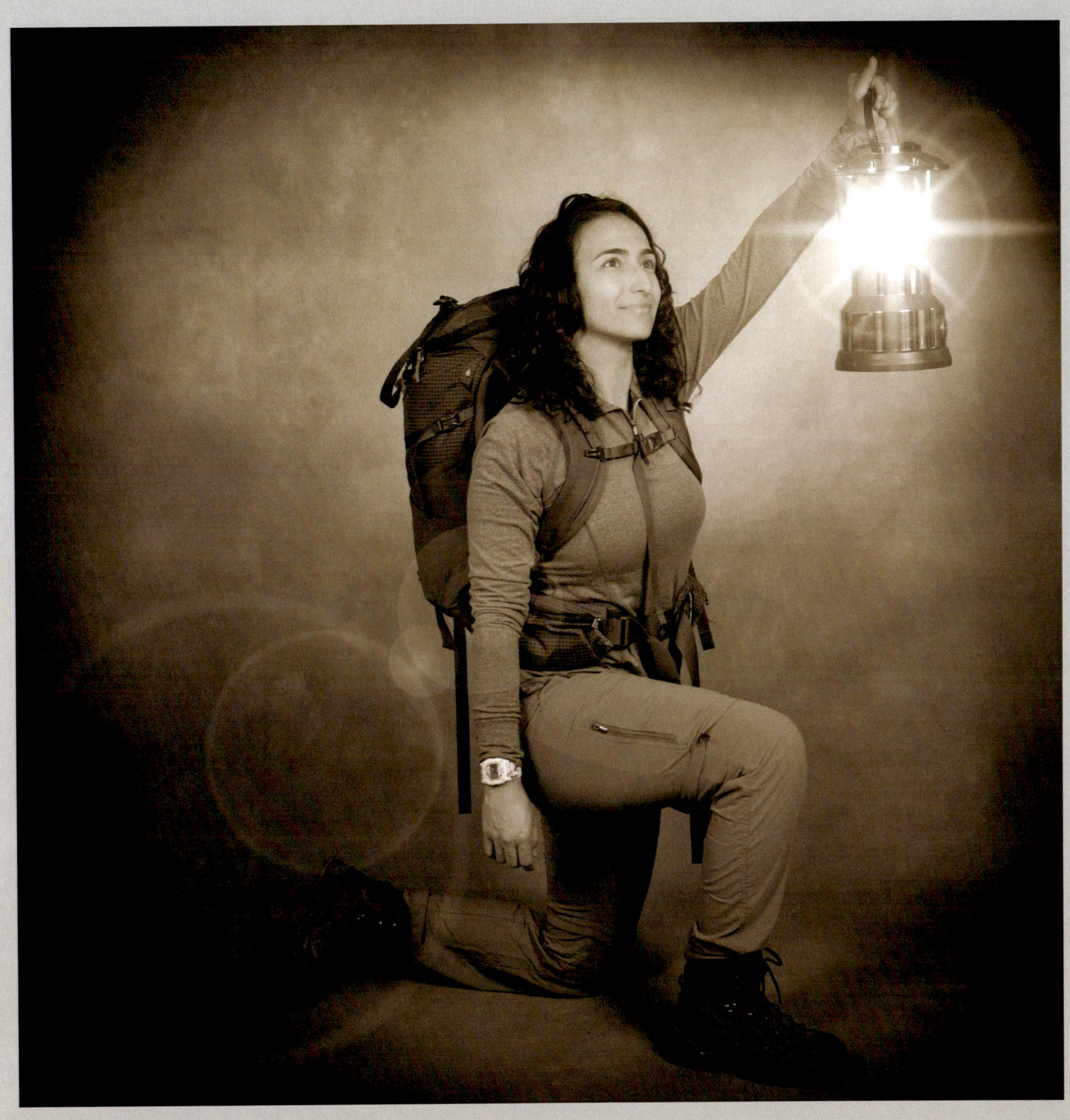

Sally De La Concha, *Library Staff.* -
"Jobs fill your pockets, but adventures fill your soul." - Jaime Lyn Beatty

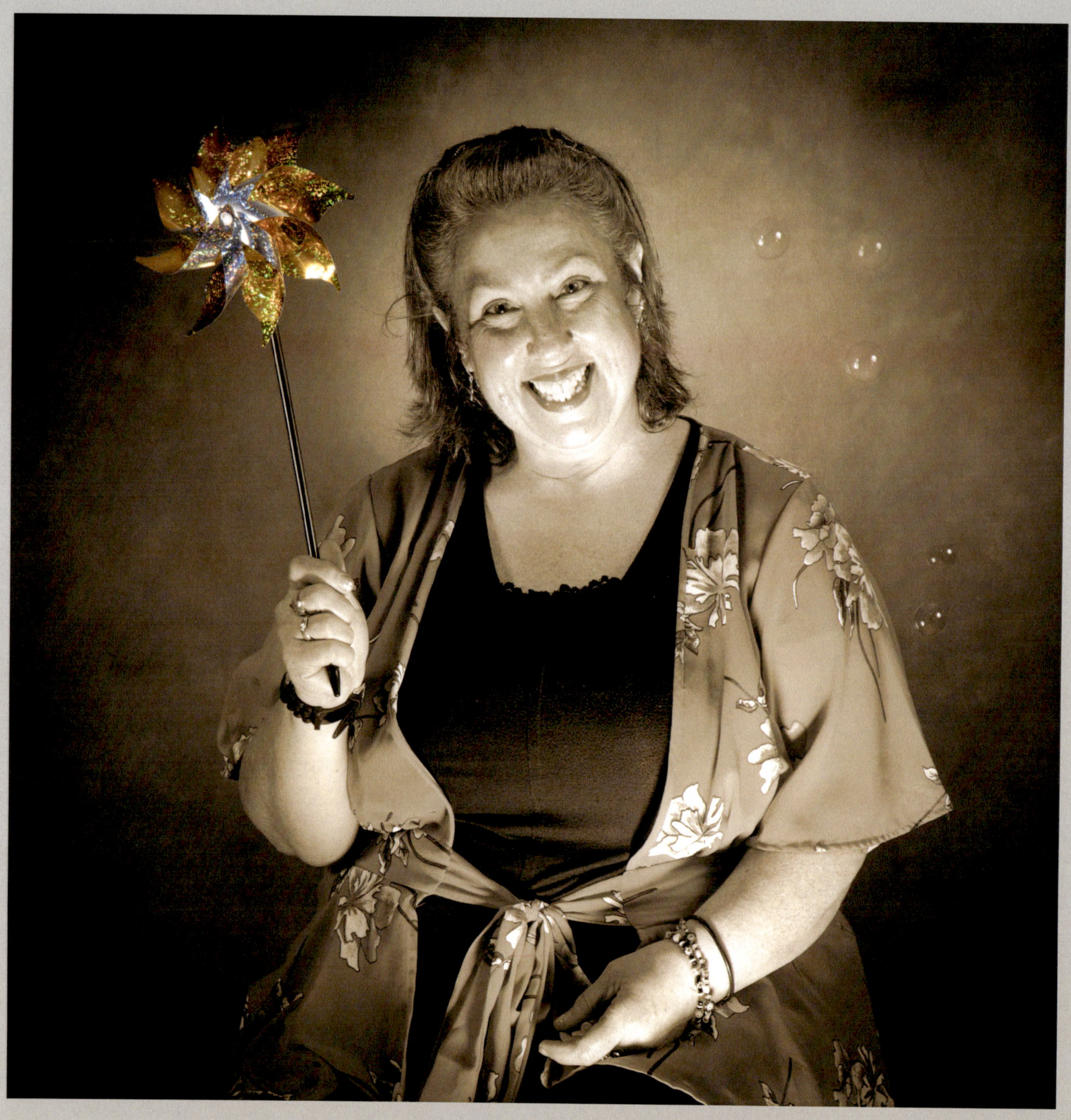

Stephanie Wack, *Soleado Elementary Teacher*. -
"Be Silly. Be Honest, Be Kind ... the world will be a better place to live!"

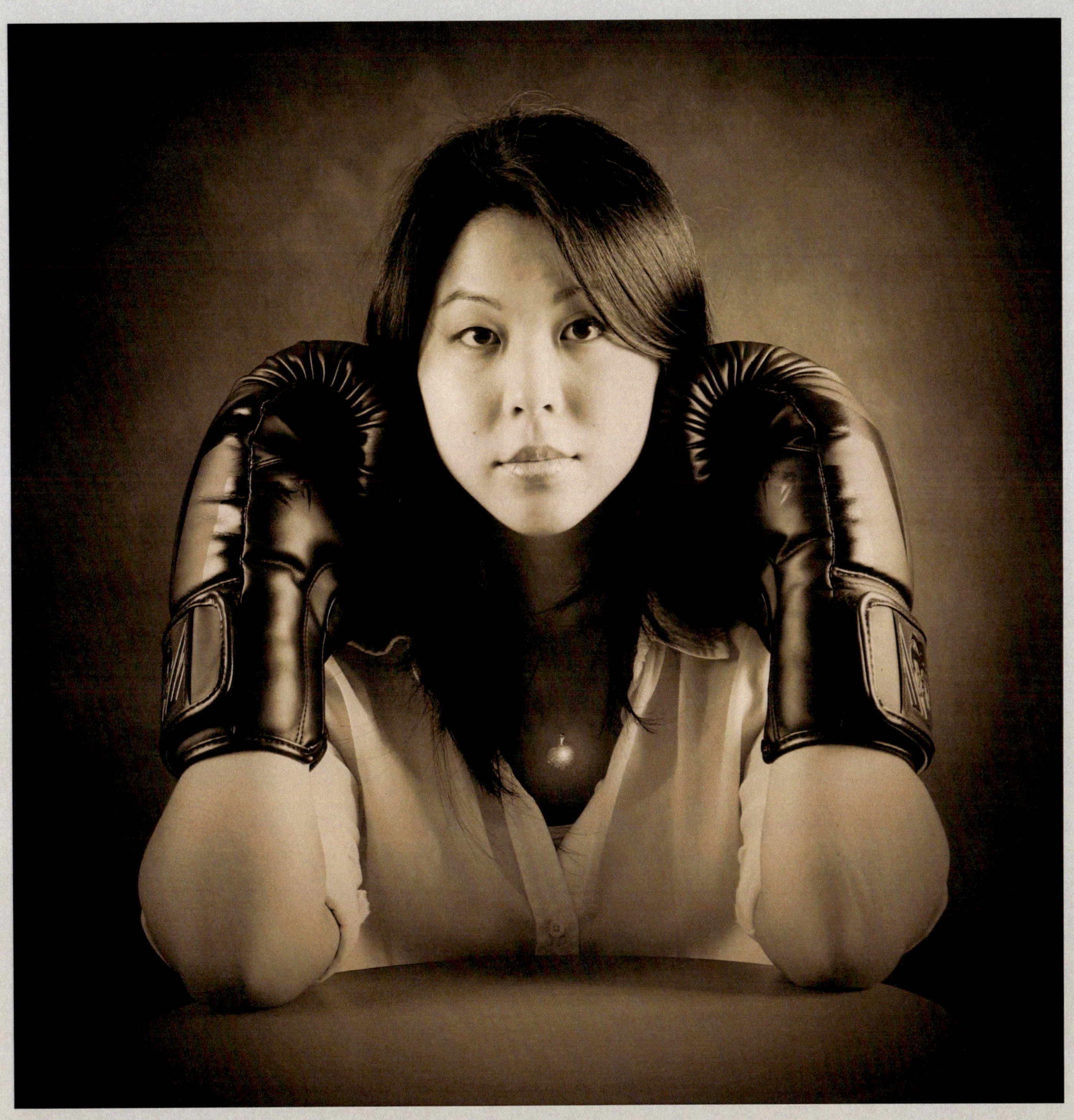

Pia-Marie Kawagoe, *Spanish Language Teacher.* -
"You're braver than you believe, stronger than you seem, and smarter than you think."
- A.A. Milne, *Winnie-the-Pooh*

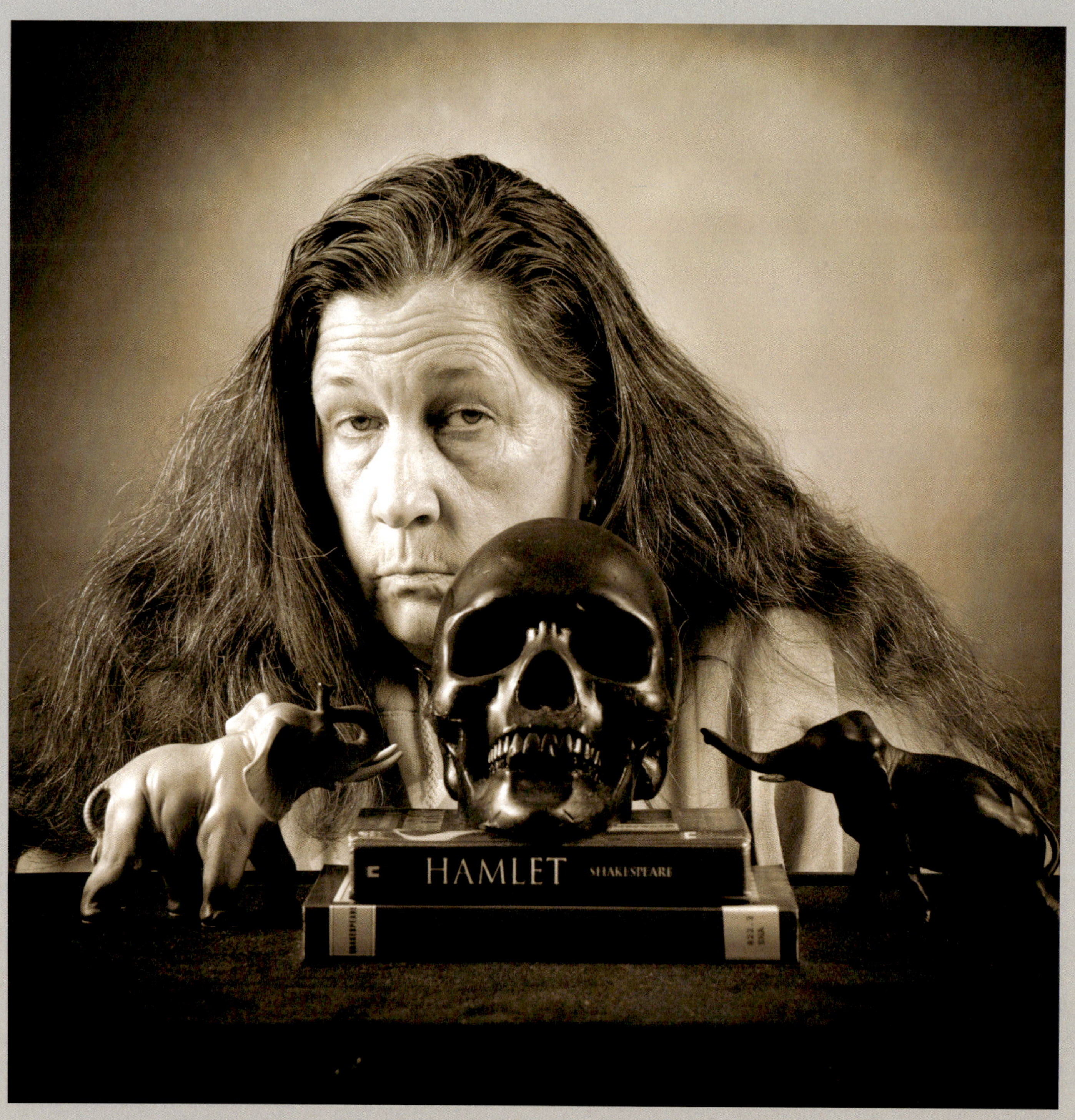

Cynthia Croft, *Ediucation Specialist & Resource Teacher.* -
"To be, not to seem." - Cicero

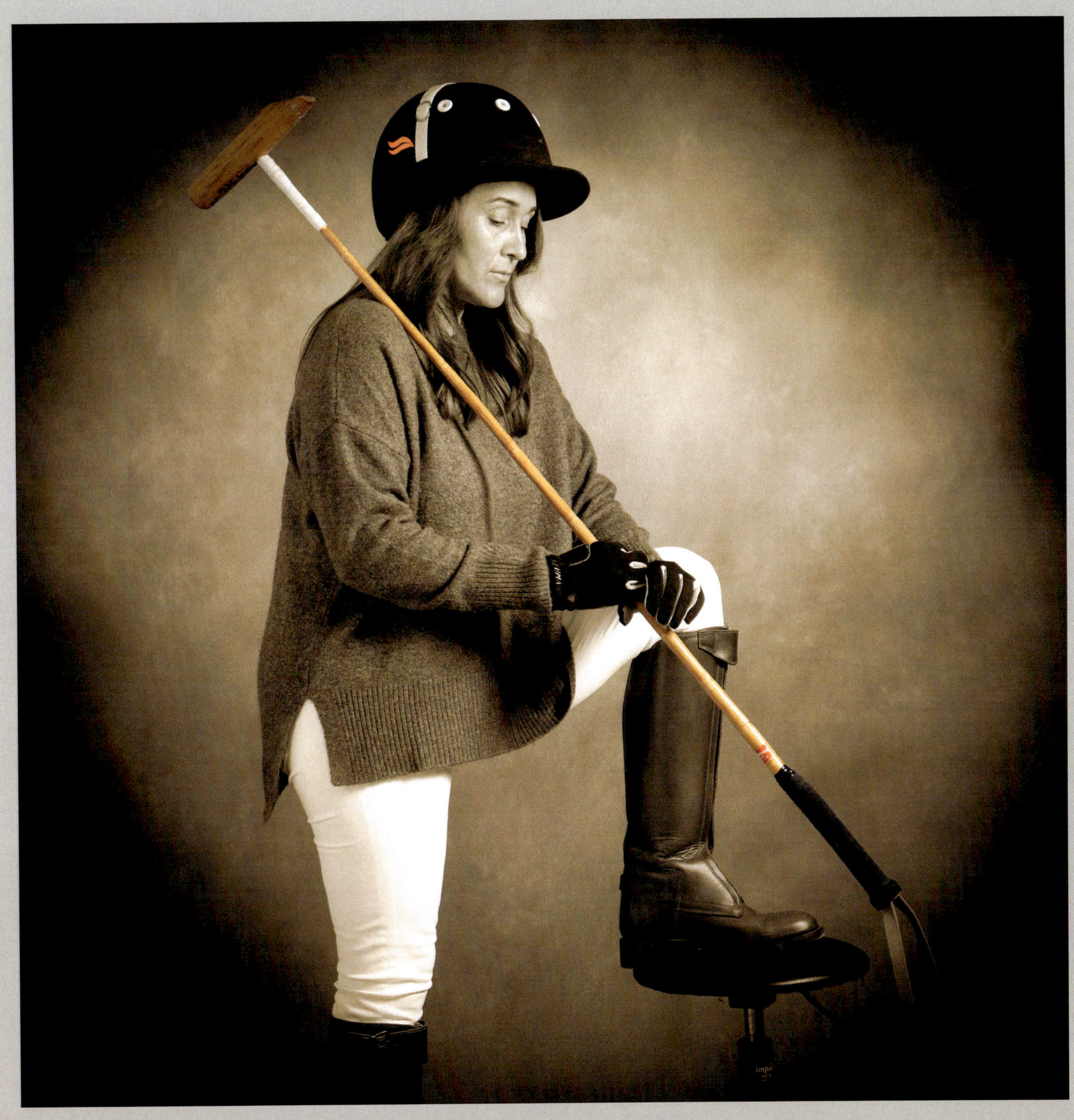

Regina Corwin, *Associate Principal.* -
"A polo pony is like a motorbike with a mind of its own weighing half a ton." -
Anonymous

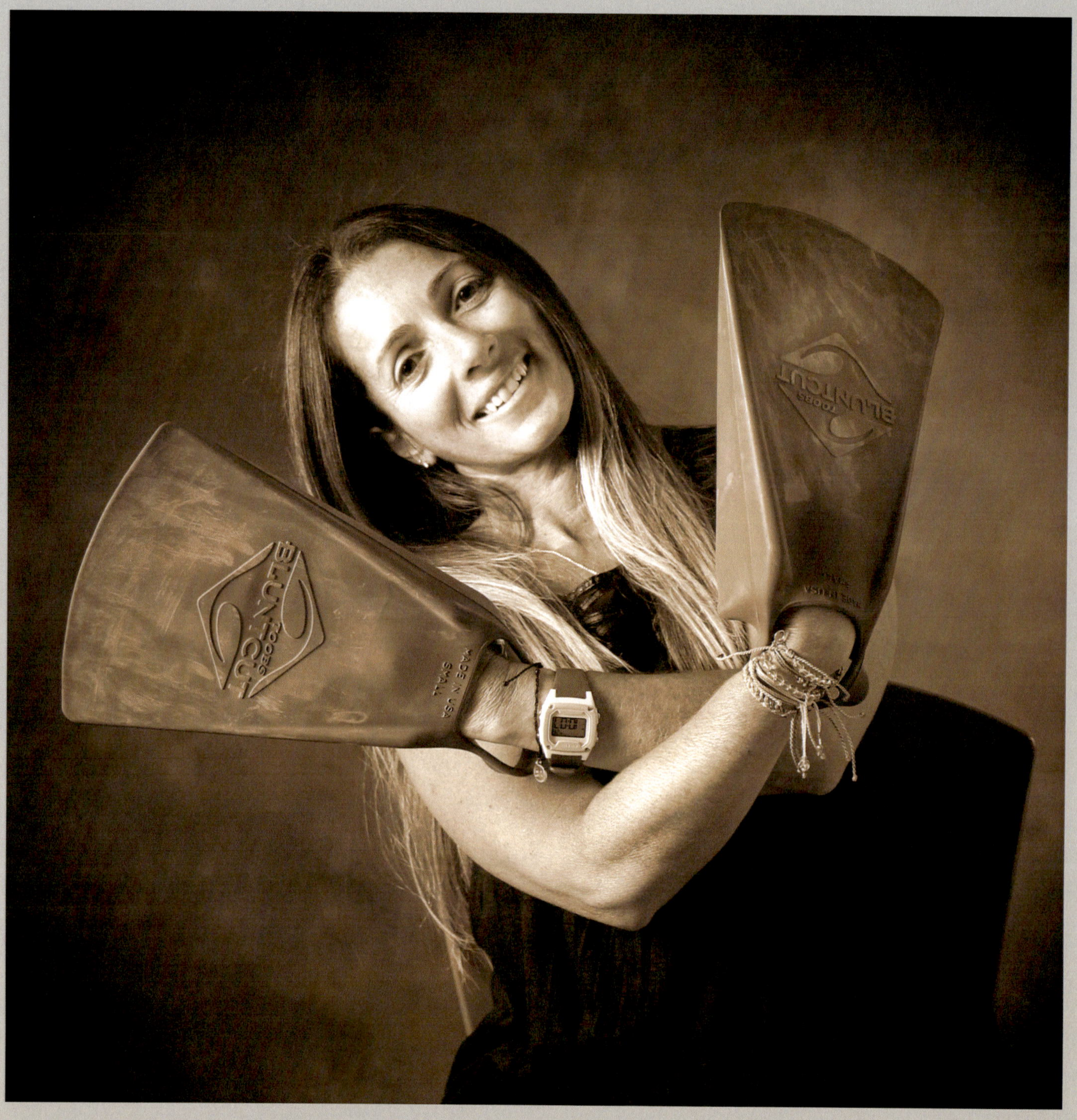

Patricia Heimrich, *Study Skills Teacher.* -
"Always be yourself unless you can be a mermaid, then be a mermaid."

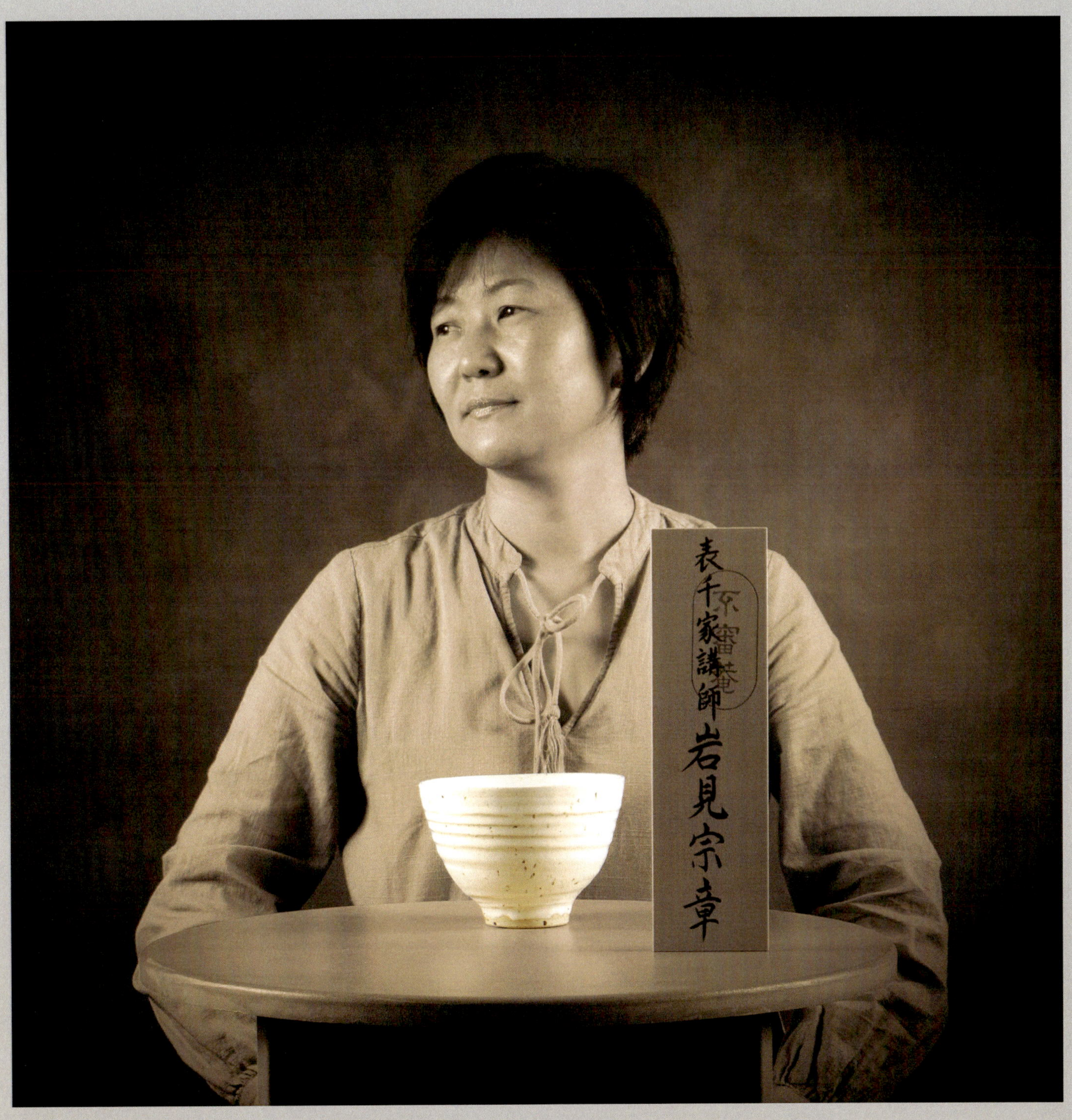

Sachiko Iwami, *Japanese Language Teacher.* -
"Every day is a good day." - Yun Men (Zen Master)

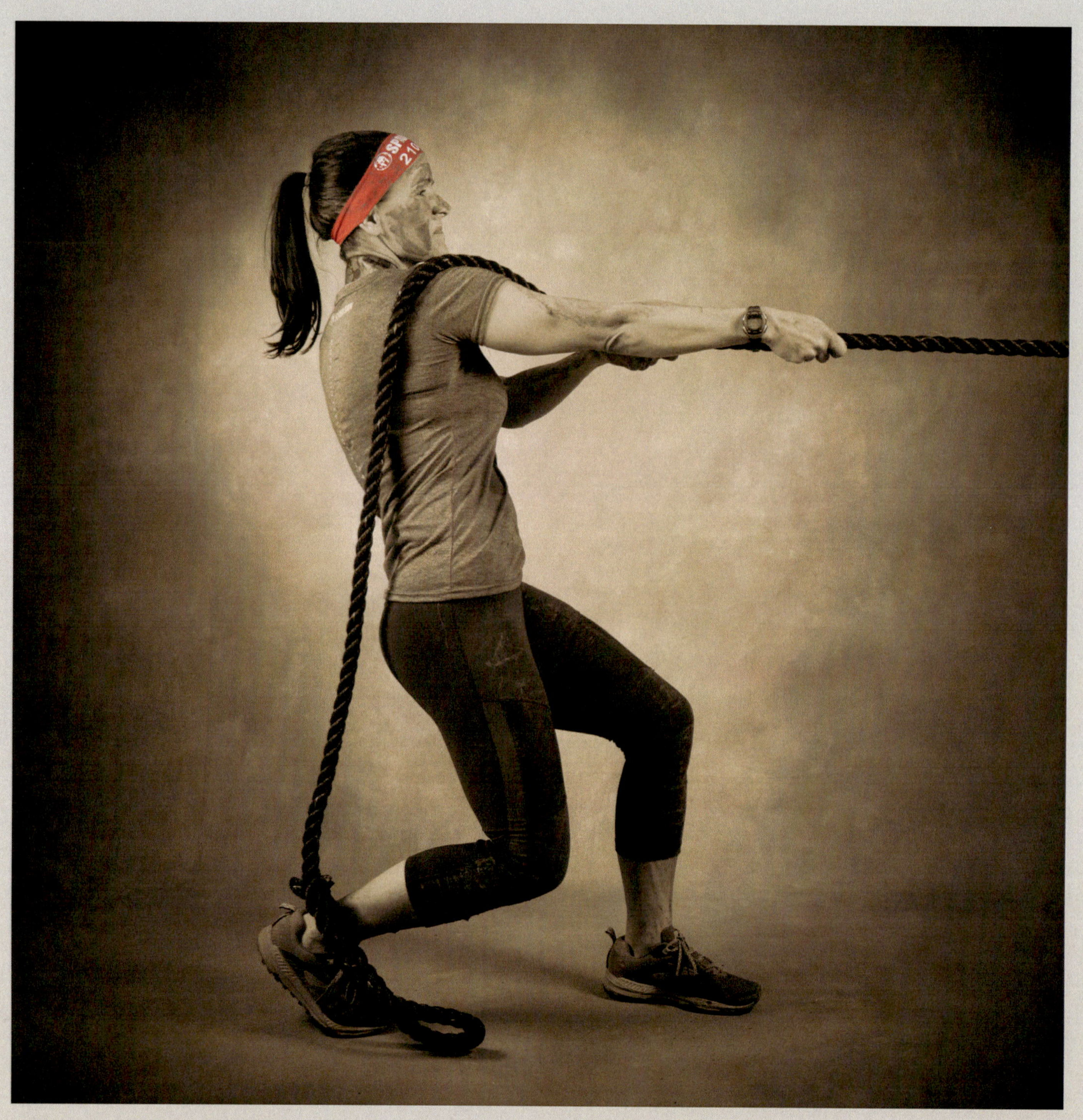

Sandra Sidella, *English Language Teacher.*

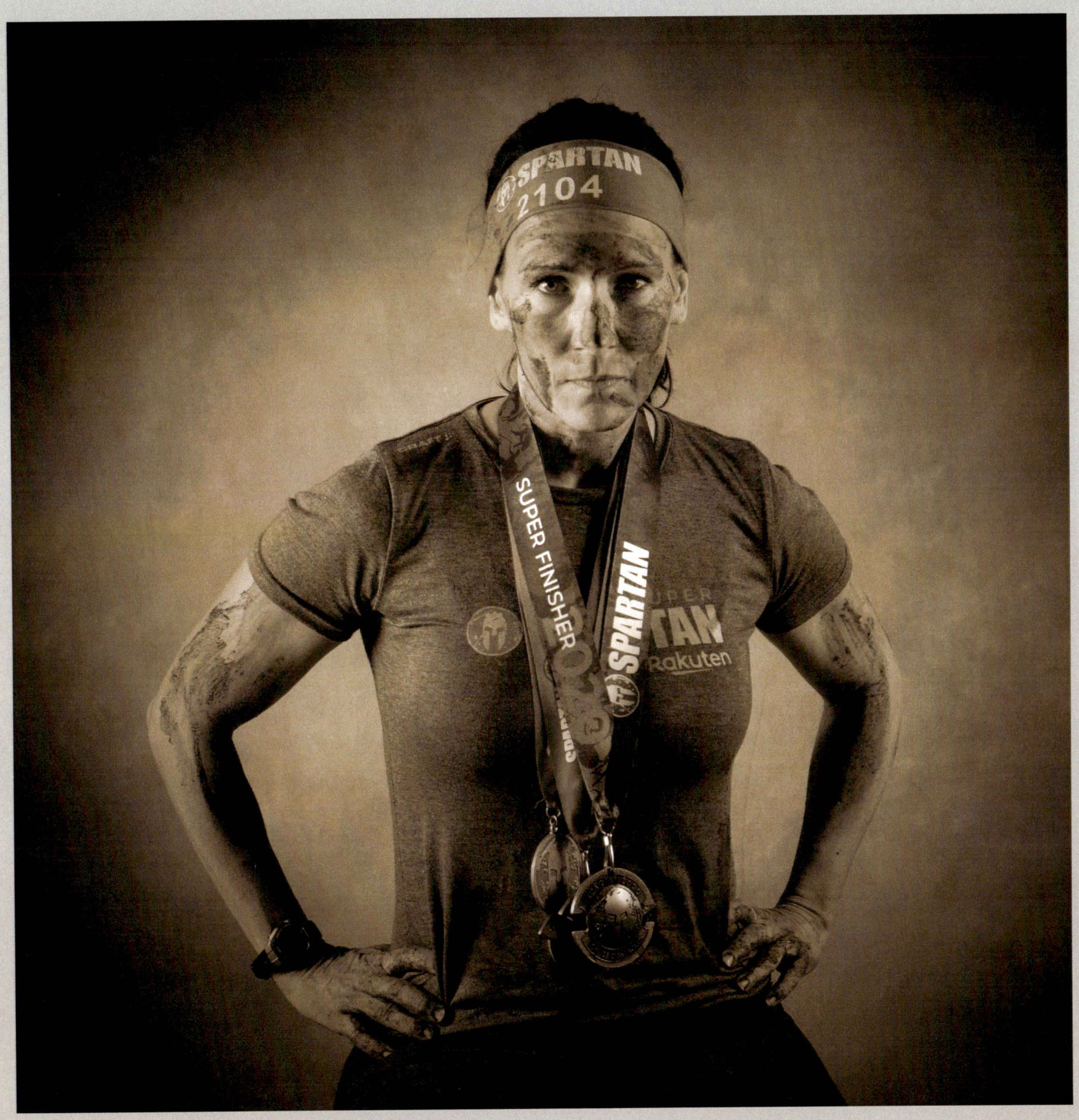

Sandra Sidella, *English Language Teacher.* -
"I will never be the woman with the perfect hair, who can wear white and not spill on it." -
Carrie Bradshaw.
"Nor would I want to." - Sandi Sidella

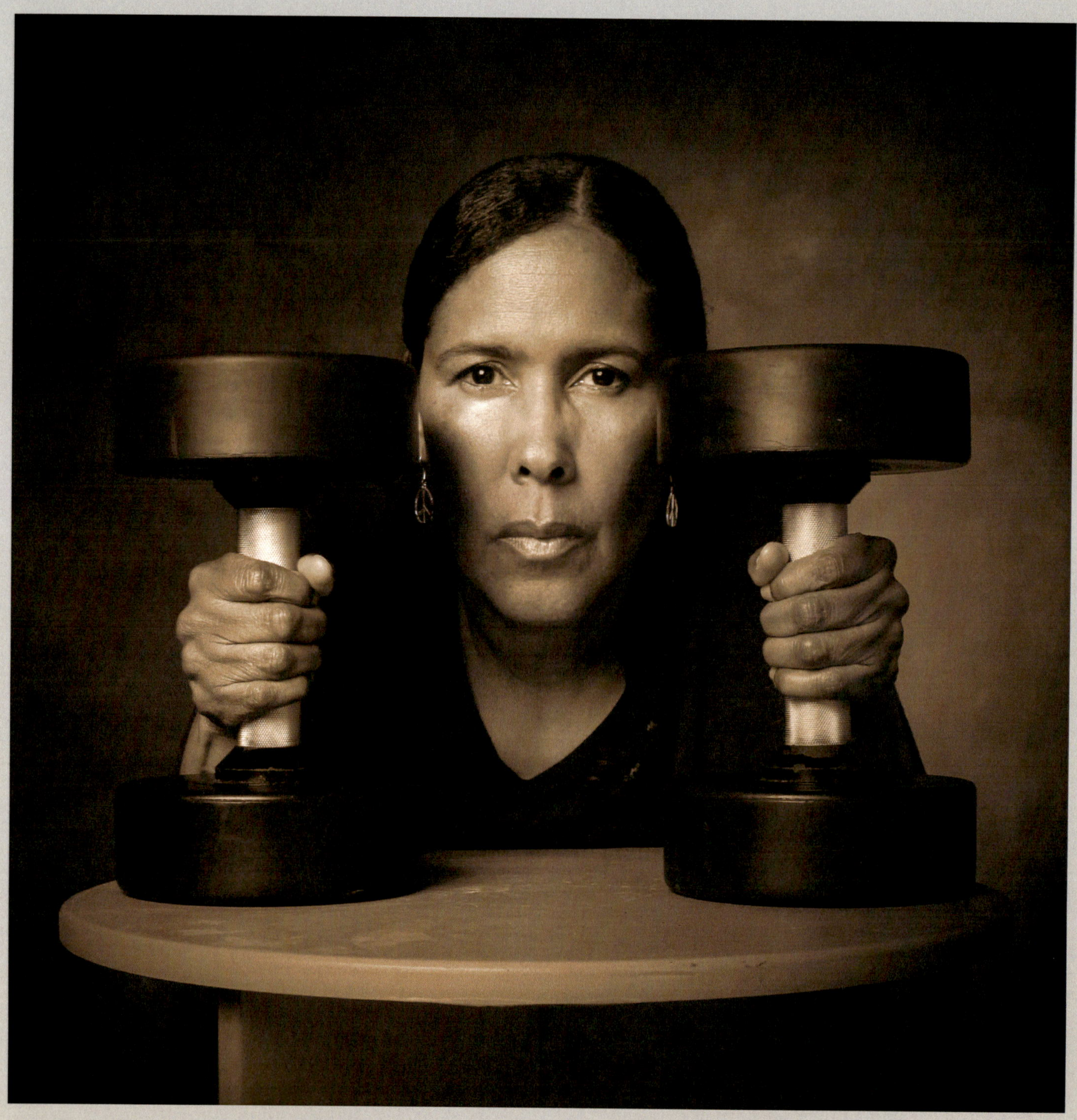

Velvet Thompson, *Security Guard.* -
"Strength = Consistency"

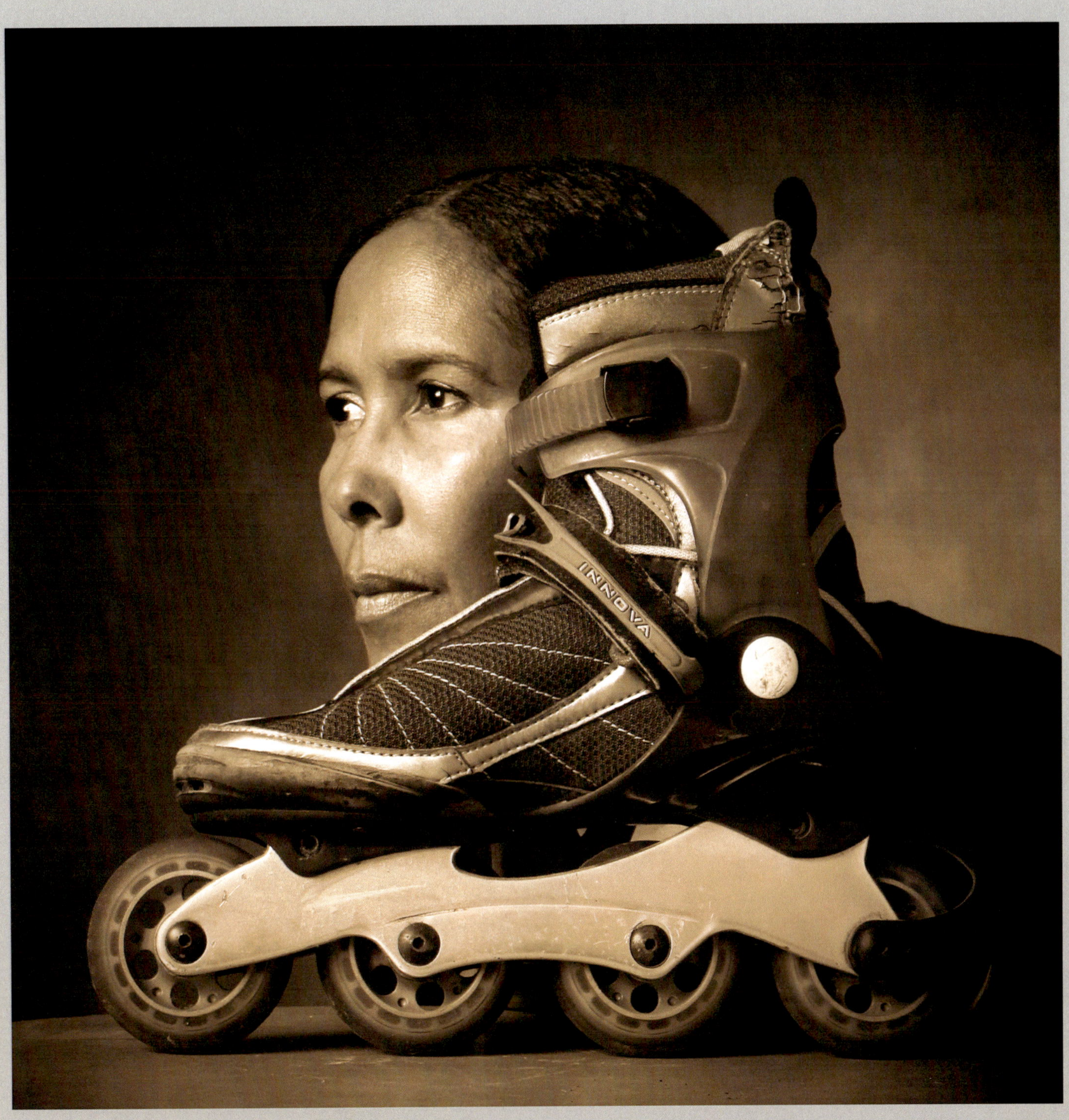

Velvet Thompson, *Security Guard.* -
"Challenging Boundaries"

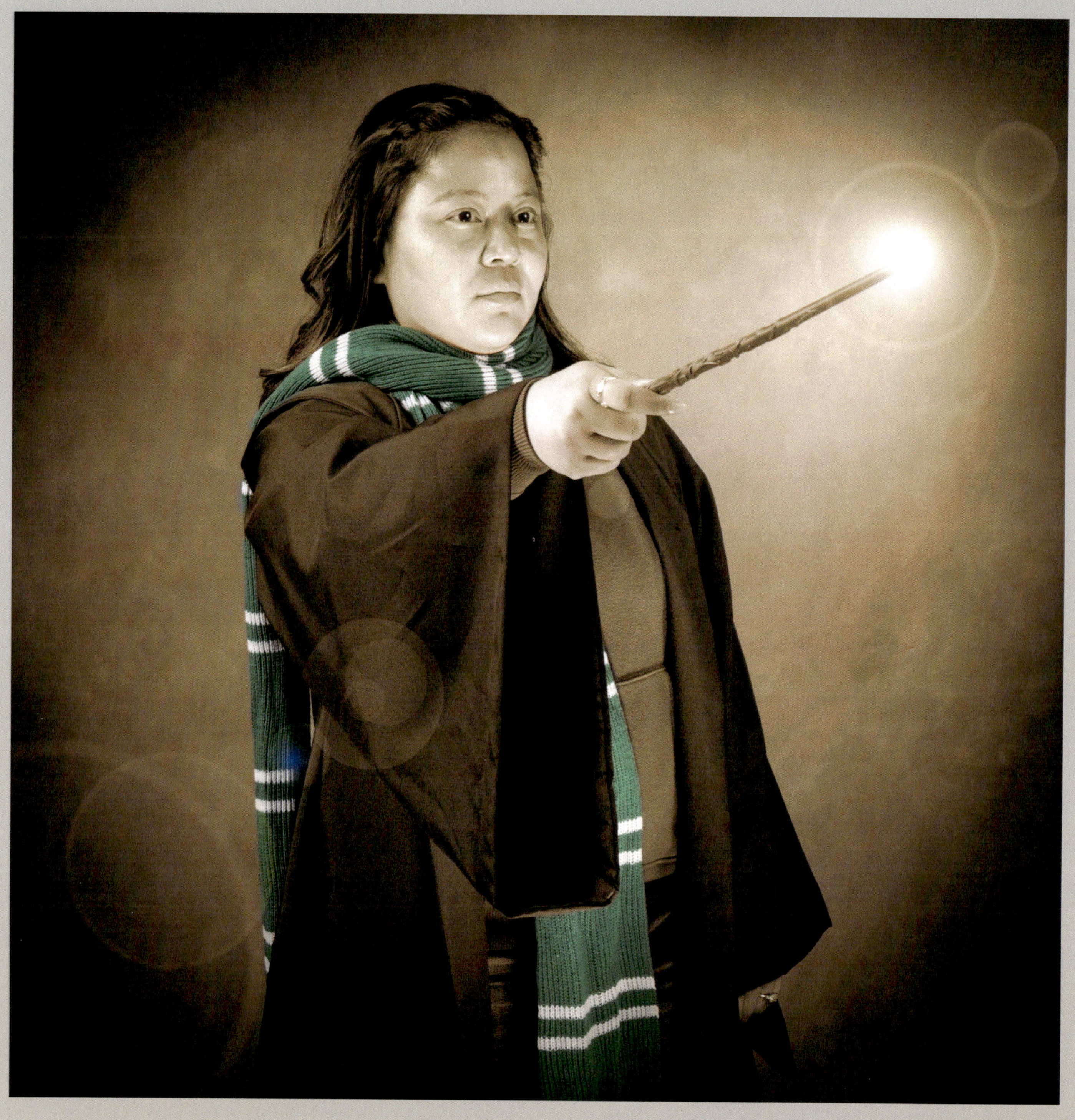

Soriya Neung, *Attendance Staff.* -
"Becoming me was the greatest creative project of my life." - Lev Grossman, *The Magicians*

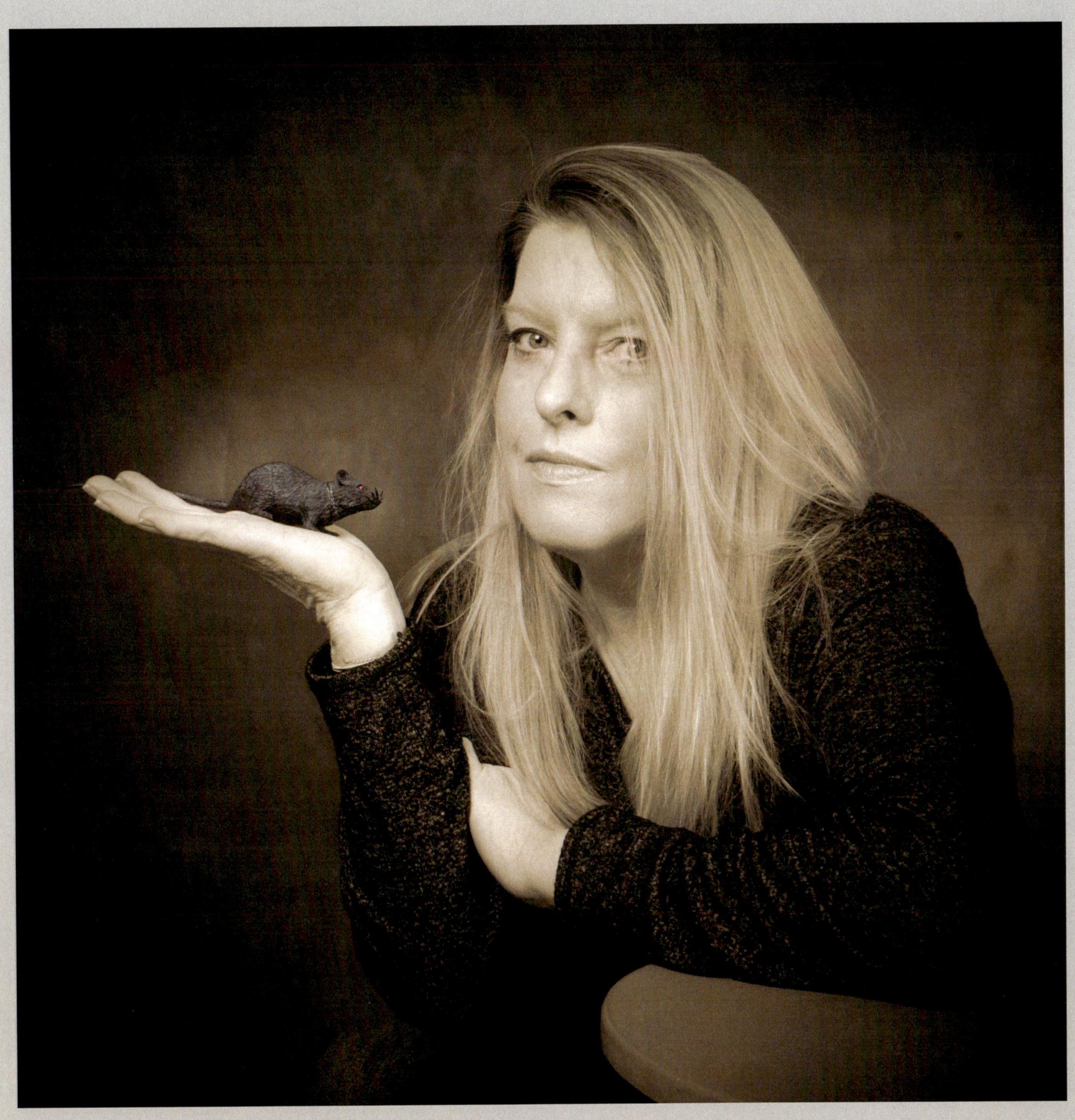

Vicki Croucier, *Student Store & Wife of RATT Band Base Player.* -
"Like Geico I also have a Ratt problem."

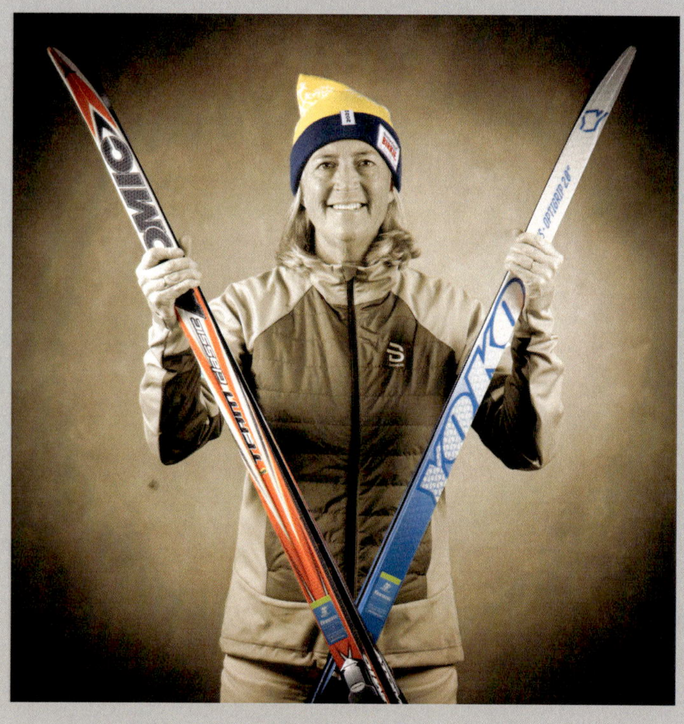

Barbara DeWitt, *English Language Teacher.*

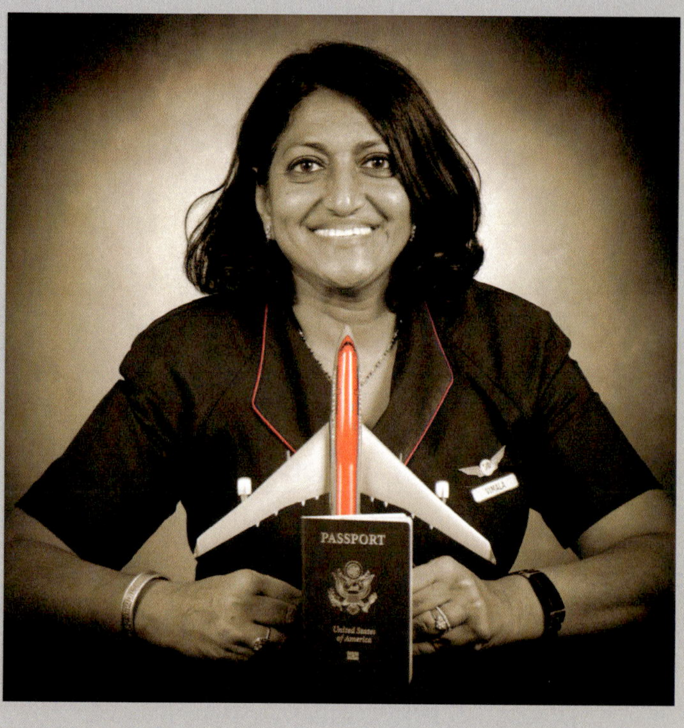

Vimala Velayutha, *Student Aide.* -
"Some people just know how to fly."

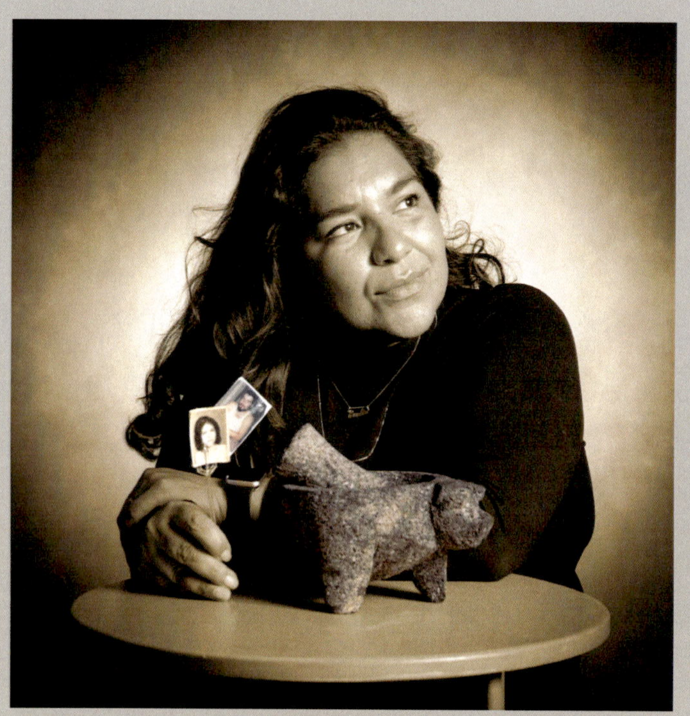

Evelin Recinos, *Soleado Elementary Teacher.*

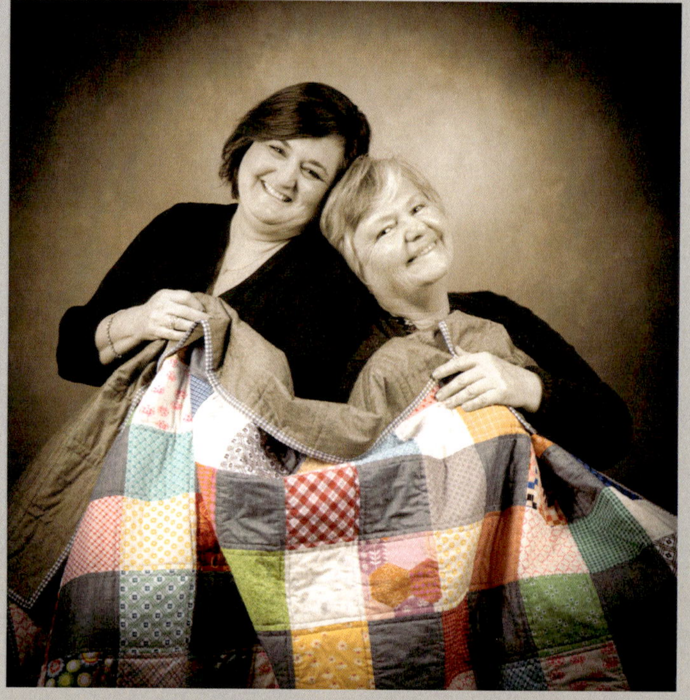

Julie Arico & Nancy Shafer, *College Career Center.* -
"Mother's hold their children's hands for a short while, but their hearts forever."

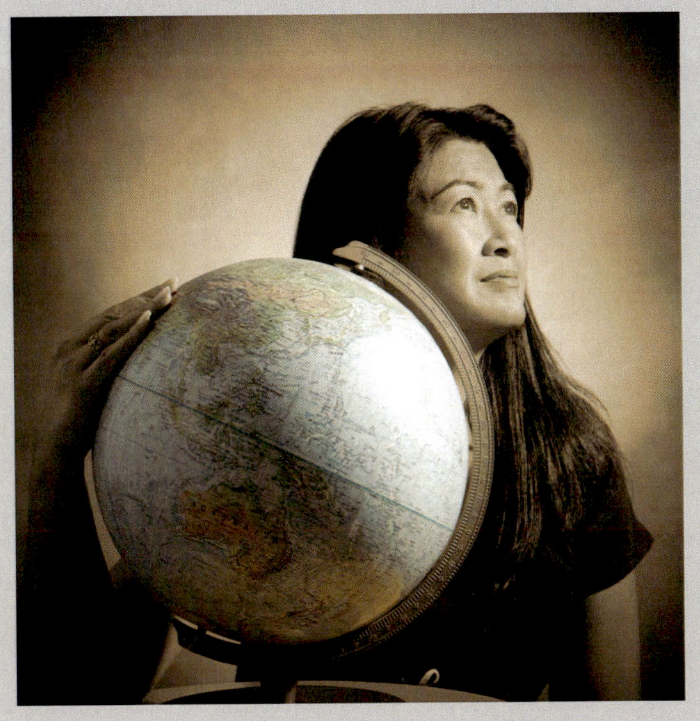 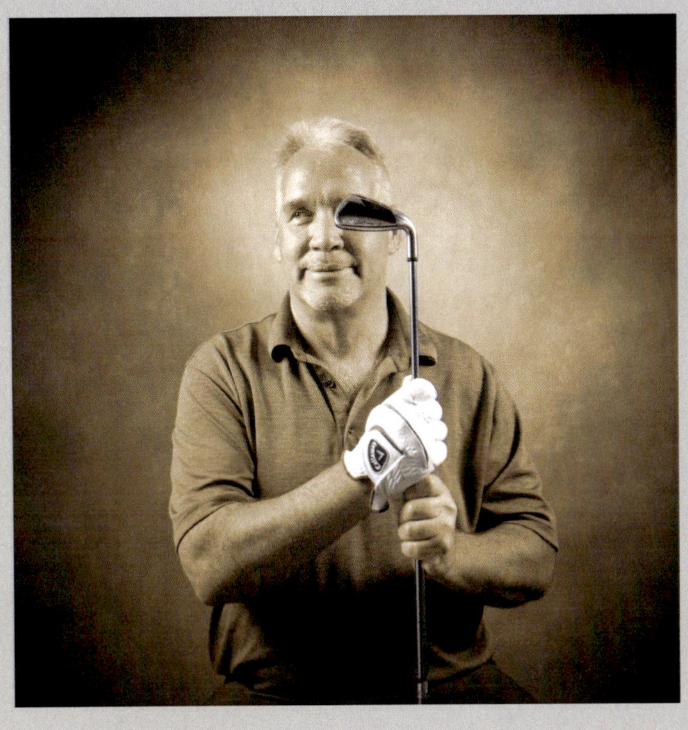

Mary-Ann Chacon, *Nurse's Assistant.*

Kevin Nowacki, *PVPUSD Plumber.*

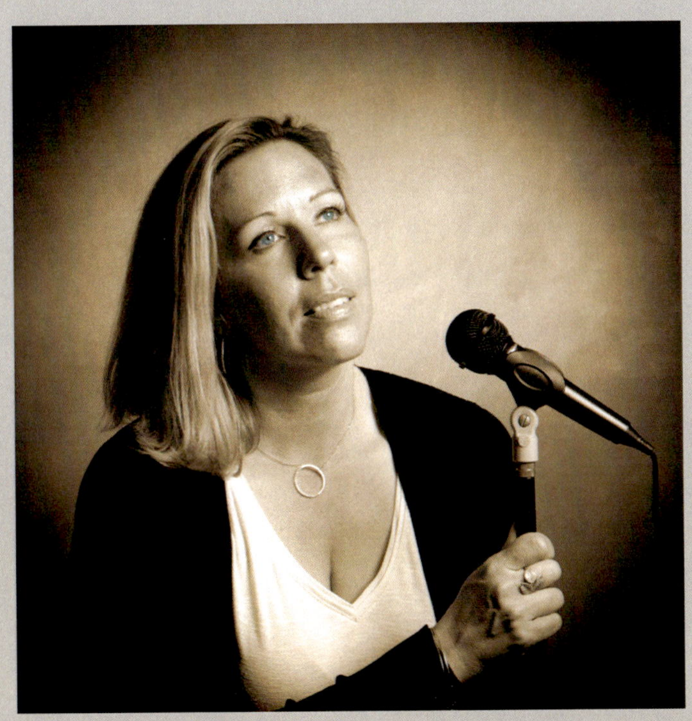 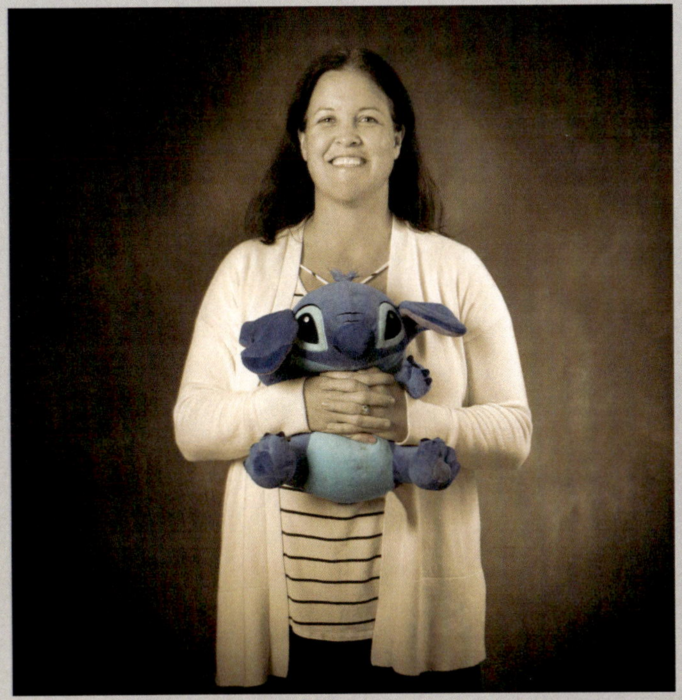

C.C. Hvlac, *Principal at Soleado Elementary.* -
"Use your voice for good."

Jennifer Panagos, *Associate Principal.* -
"To succeed students need more than content knowledge - they need to see themselves as efficacious learners."

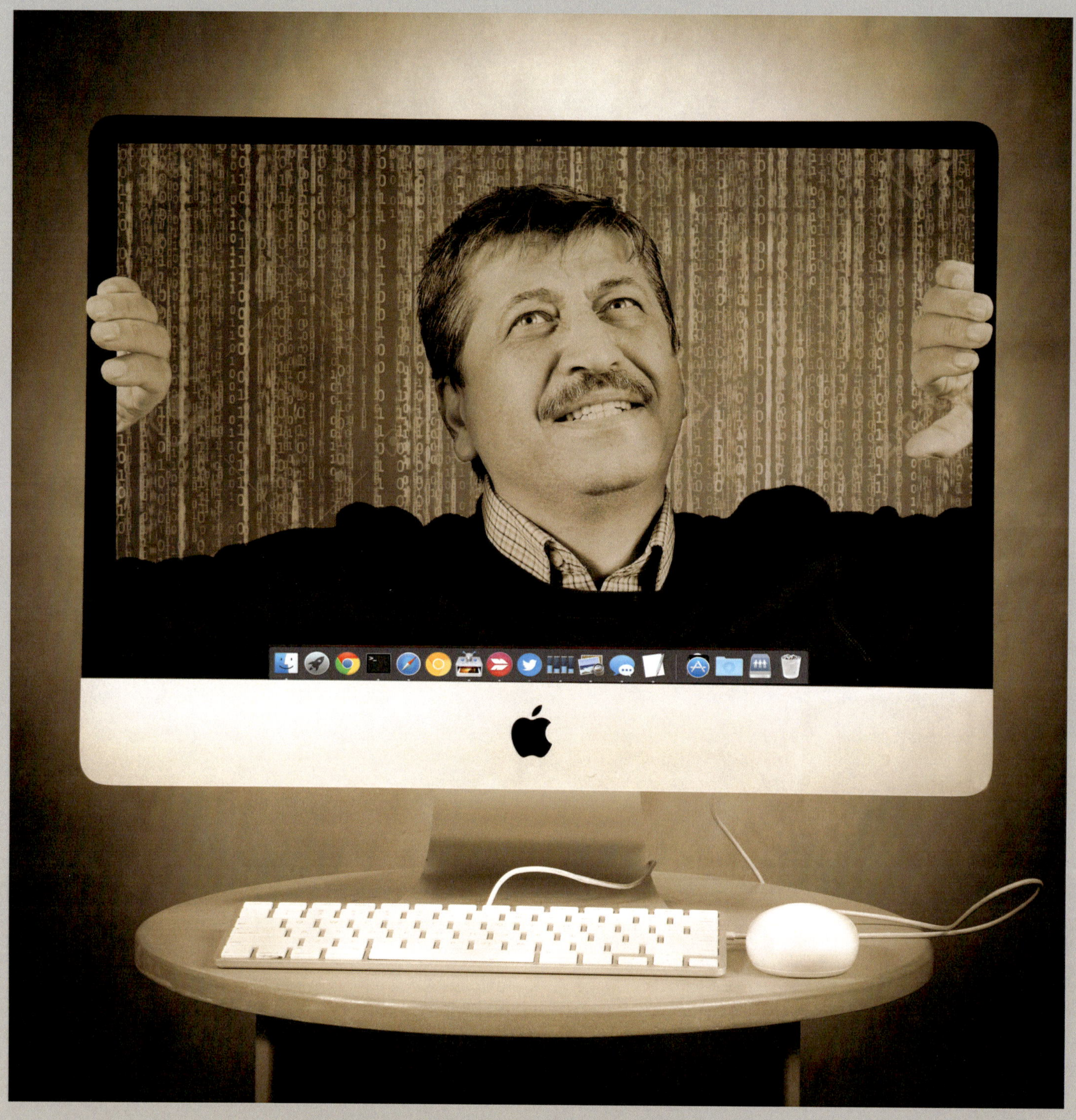

Hassan Twiet, *Computer Science & Engineering Teacher.* -
"Good better best never let rest until the good becomes better and the better becomes best."

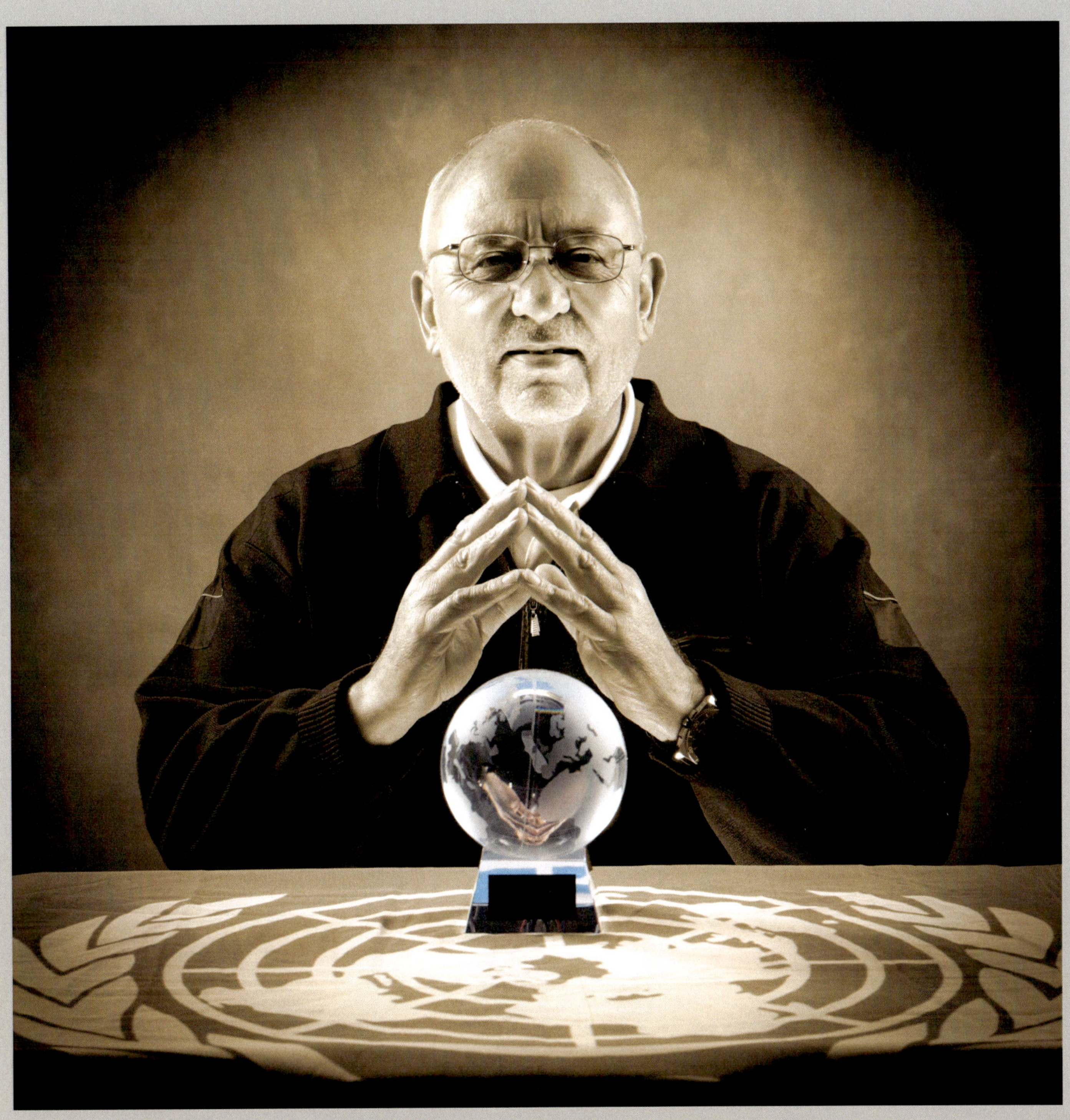

Jim Dimitriou, *Mock United Nations Director.* -
"We shall not cease from exploration, and the end of all our exploring will be to arrive where we started and know the place for the first time." T.S. Elliot.

CONTENTS